CW00741523

So you really want to learn

LATIN

TRANSLATIONS

GALORE PARK

So you really want to learn
LATIN
TRANSLATIONS

Betty Halifax M.A. (Cantab.)
Series Editor: Nicholas Oulton M.A. (Oxon.)

GALORE PARK

Published by Galore Park Publishing Ltd., 3 Crown Yard, Bedgebury Estate, Goudhurst, Kent TN17 2QZ

Text copyright © Betty Halifax 2001

Illustrations copyright © Ian Douglass 2001

Typography and layout by S&B Associates, Nymet Rowland, Crediton, Devon EX17 6AN

Printed and bound by Biddles Limited, Guildford, GU1 1DA

ISBN 1 902984 07 2

First published 2001

AUTHOR'S FOREWORD

This reader has been written to accompany Book 1 of *So you really want to learn Latin*, published by Galore Park. However it should be of use to anyone of any age in the early stages of learning Latin, as the chapter headings show which aspect of grammar is being emphasised and the comprehensive vocabulary should prevent any difficulties for those teaching themselves or working at home.

B.H.
July 2001

ACKNOWLEDGEMENTS

I should like to thank Nick Oulton not only for suggesting that I write this reader but also for his helpful and practical ideas for presentation of the material. Thanks are also due to Stephen Anderson and Theo Zinn for their meticulous and scholarly checking of the text, for which I am very grateful. Any errors which remain are, of course, my own.

Contents

CHAPTER 1
Verbs: the 1st conjugation and sum

Introduction

When you first begin learning Latin you may often think that the Romans were a weird lot, perpetually changing the endings of words just to annoy you. But they weren't thinking of *you* when they wrote and spoke, but of each other, and they obviously thought they had a first-rate method of communicating. If they had been learning English they would have thought *we* were the weird lot, having to use so many words when it wasn't necessary.

Each time you learn a new ending you will see more clearly how their minds worked. You might even begin to agree with them about their language! But learning Latin is like learning most things: you need practice if you are going to be good at it. Here it is!

Welcome to The Underworld!

Many Romans believed that after death one's spirit went to the Underworld, reached only by crossing the River Styx. There the seriously wicked might be directed to Tartarus, a place of punishment, while the seriously virtuous might end up in the Elysian Fields, a place of happiness. The fate of new arrivals was in the hands of three judges: Minos, Rhadamanthus and Aeacus. Living people were not allowed (except very occasionally) to enter the Underworld and the entrance was surrounded by weird creatures and was very well-guarded.

In the following passages we introduce you to four of the Underworld's most famous "tourist attractions". Try to work out who or what they are by studying the questions and answers. Clues to some of the words you may not know are given below each passage.

Our first few passages involve the use of questions. Adding *-ne* to the first word in a Latin sentence turns it into a question.

> *Amant* = they love; *amantne*? = Do they love?
>
> *Vocat* = he calls; *vocatne*? = Does he call?

Nothing too tricky there, then!

1

"Tourist attraction" no. 1

Q. *cantāsne?*
A. *nōn cantō.*

Q. *cantāvistīne?*
A. *nōn cantāvī. nōn cantō. numquam cantābō.*

Q. *vocāsne?*
A. *nōn vocō, sed saepe sonō et saepe sonābō.*

Q. *quōmodo sonās?*
A. *lātrō. saepe lātrō. lātrō et lātrō et lātrō.*

Q. *lātrās et lātrās et lātrās?*
A. *lātrō et lātrō et lātrō.*

Q. *quis es?*
A. *nōn nārrābō.*

Vocabulary

cantō, -āre	=	I sing
lātrō, -āre	=	I bark
nārrō, -āre	=	I tell
nōn	=	not
numquam	=	never
quis?	=	who?
quōmodo?	=	how?
saepe	=	often
vocō, -āre	=	I call

The verb 'to be'

sum	I am
es	You are
est	He/she/it is
sumus	We are
estis	You are
sunt	They are

Detective work

Many words and phrases which you meet in Latin can be successfully worked out, particularly if you use your brains and look out for clues:

cantāsne? If *cantās* = you are singing, and *-ne* makes it a question, what must *cantāsne* mean?

sonās If something is **resonant**, it makes a loud…

quis es? If *quis* = who and *es* = you are, what must *quis es* mean?

N.B. As well as being able to cope with regular verbs like *amō*, in this chapter you need to know the irregular verb *sum* (see above). For those of you who know French, it is similar to the verb *être* (don't forget that Gaul was the largest province of the Roman Empire).

"Tourist attraction" no. 2

Q. *quis es?*
A. *nōn nārrābō.*

Q. *lātrāsne?*
A. *nōn lātrō.*

Q. *lātrāvistīne?*
A. *numquam lātrāvī.*

Q. *labōrāsne?*
A. *semper labōrō. semper labōrāvī et semper labōrābō.*

Q. *quōmodo labōrās?*
A. *rēmigō. semper rēmigō et semper rēmigābō.*

Q. *cūr rēmigās?*
A. (Pointing to a group of shadowy figures on the shore) *ecce, appropinquant! intrant! semper appropinquant et semper appropinquābunt. semper intrant et semper intrābunt. rēmigō et semper rēmigābō.*

Q. *quis es?*
A. *nōn nārrābō.*

Vocabulary

appropinquō, -āre	= I approach
cūr?	= why?
ecce!	= look!
intrō, -āre	= I enter
labōrō, -āre	= I work
rēmigō, -āre	= I row
semper	= always

Dead and buried

When a Roman died his friends or family would place a coin in his mouth. This was payment for the ferryman, Charon, whose job it was to row the souls of the dead across the River Styx and into the Underworld; no coin, no crossing. Once on the other side the souls had to get past Cerberus, the three-headed dog who guarded the Underworld for his master, Pluto, the god of the Dead.

"Tourist attraction" no. 3

Q. *quis es?*

A. *nōn nārrābō.*

Q. *peccāvistīne?*

A. *peccāvī.*

Q. *quōmodo peccāvistī?*

A. *necāvī... necāvī...ēheu! (lacrimat). nōn dīvulgābō.*

Q. *fortasse Iuppiter tē nōn amat?*

A. *Iuppiter mē nōn amat. numquam mē amābit. (lacrimat.)*

Q. *cūr lacrimās?*

A. *lacrimō quod Iuppiter mē accūsāvit et mē damnāvit.*

Q. *quōmodo Iuppiter tē damnāvit?*

A. *pōtāre volō: nōn pōtō. cēnāre volō: nōn cēnō. Iuppiter mē vetat. nec cēnābō nec pōtābō! ēheu!*

Vocabulary

amō, -āre	= I love, like
cēnō, -āre	= I dine
ēheu!	= alas!
fortasse	= perhaps
lacrimō, -āre	= I weep
nec...nec	= neither...nor
necō, -āre	= I kill
peccō, -āre	= I sin
quod	= because
*volō**	= I wish

* This is an irregular verb. Don't panic, just translate it!

Detective work

dīvulgābō	We get the word divulge from this.
mē, tē	It should be pretty easy to work out what these pronouns mean. They're the same in French, if that helps.
accūsāvit, damnāvit	Which English words do we get from these?
pōtāre	What does one do with a **potion**? In French, what does *eau non* **potable** mean?
vetat	If one puts a veto on something, what is one doing?

"Tourist attraction" no. 4

Q. *quis es?*
A. *nōn nārrābō.*

Q. *cantāsne?*
A. *cantō.*

Q. *cantāsne saepe?*
A. *saepe cantō.*

Q. *habitāsne hīc?*
A. *hīc nōn habitō sed, ēheu! Eurydicē hīc nunc habitat. semper lacrimābam, semper, semper. Eurydicē hīc habitābat et tandem vīsitāvī. Plūtō mē vetābat retrō spectāre, sed tandem, spectāvī! ēheu! Eurydicē hīc habitat et semper hīc habitābit. semper lacrimābō, semper, semper…*

Vocabulary

habitō, -āre	= I live
hīc	= here
nunc	= now
retrō	= backwards
spectō, -āre	= I watch, look at
tandem	= at last

Orpheus and Eurydice

The story of Orpheus and Eurydice is one of the most touching tales in antiquity. Orpheus, the musician whose skill with the lyre allowed him to charm the birds, tame wild animals, even prevent clashing rocks from clashing, was married to the beautiful wood nymph Eurydice. When Eurydice was chased through a wood by the satyr Silenus, and died of a snake wound, Orpheus was distraught and refused to give her up. He entered the realm of Pluto and begged him to release his wife. The king was unmoved by his pleas, but Pluto's wife, Proserpina, persuaded him to take pity on the musician. Orpheus was thus allowed to take his wife out of the Underworld, out to the land of the living; on one condition: he must not look back at his wife until she was safely out of Pluto's kingdom.

The journey away from Pluto's dark halls was long and lonely. Orpheus had to trust the king of the dead, for he could not turn round to look on his beloved wife. He had to trust that she was following him; but was she? He longed to turn and check that she was there. He longed to know if his wife was really with him once more.

In the end, just as he reached the furthest limits of Pluto's kingdom, and was within a few paces of safety, he turned. Eurydice immediately vanished before his eyes, and returned to the land of the dead. Orpheus was alone again, this time for ever. He never played his lyre again and was soon to die, alone and despised, beaten to death by a tribe of wild hill women.

CHAPTER 2
1st declension nouns

In Chapter 2 we concentrate on nouns. At first it seems strange that they keep changing their endings but you will soon get used to it. All you need is practice.

Jupiter rules okay!

The gods of Mount Olympus were ruled by Jupiter, the thunderer. If he was displeased he would hurl a thunderbolt at whoever or whatever displeased him. Alongside him were other gods and goddesses, brothers, sisters and children of the king, who all had various responsibilities. Here are some of them:

Iuppiter rēgnat!

Iūnō est dea mātrōnārum.

Minerva sapientiam et pugnās cūrat.

Cerēs agricultūram cūrat.

Dĭāna est lūna. sagittās et silvās amat.

Vocabulary

dea, -ae, f.	= goddess
pugna, -ae, f.	= battle
rēgnō, -āre	= I reign
sagitta, -ae, f.	= arrow
sapientia, -ae, f.	= wisdom
silva, -ae, f.	= a wood

Detective work

Iuppiter	Note that the king of the gods has two 't's in Latin but only one in English.
mātrōnārum	What is the English equivalent?
cūrat	A **curator** has the 'cūram' of a museum.
agricultūram	It's amazing how many English words come straight from the Latin.
lūna	Think of a lunar eclipse.

Neptūnus aquās et nautās cūrat.

Plūtō in terrīs tenebrārum habitat.

Vulcānus flammās incitat.

Mercurius est nūntius.

Apollō est sōl; sōl est Apollō.

Mārs pugnās cūrat.

Venus amōrem cūrat.

Vocabulary

aqua, -ae, f.	= water
incitō, -āre	= I stir up, incite
incola, -ae, m.	= inhabitant
terra, -ae, f.	= land
tenebrae, -ārum, f. pl.	= darkness

Detective work

One or two of the nouns which you meet here have unfamiliar endings. Don't worry, we will meet them properly later.

nautās	These men are interested in nautical affairs.
flammās	Think of inflammable and inflammatory.
nūntius	The noun from *nūntiō*
sōl	Think of a solar eclipse, or a solar heating system.
pugnāre	The verb from *pugna*.
amōrem	The noun from *amō*.

Quis sum?

1. *rēgīna deārum sum. mātrōnās amō et adiuvō. nymphās nōn amō quod Iuppiter nymphās amat. quis sum?*

2. *puellās et agricolās et nautās sagittīs vulnerō – et statim amant. quis sum?*

3. *dea sum et lūna sum. cervās captō. natābam et, ēheu, Actaeōn mē spectābat. quis sum?*

4. *dea sum. agricolās et agricultūram cūrō. fīliam Prŏserpinam amābam. Plūtō Prŏserpinam captāvit. quis sum?*

5. *undās aut plācō aut excitō. nautās adiuvō. quis sum?*

6. *dea sum. sapientiam cūrō. lānam et cūram lānae amō. Arachnē quoque lānam et cūram lānae amābat. Arachnē mē prŏvocāvit et exclāmāvit: 'tē superābō'. sed puellam superāvī quod dea sum. Arachnē nōn iam mē prŏvocābit. nunc arānea est! quis sum?*

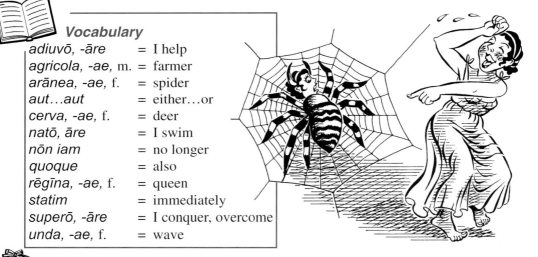

Vocabulary

adiuvō, -āre	= I help
agricola, -ae, m.	= farmer
arānea, -ae, f.	= spider
aut…aut	= either…or
cerva, -ae, f.	= deer
natō, āre	= I swim
nōn iam	= no longer
quoque	= also
rēgīna, -ae, f.	= queen
statim	= immediately
superō, -āre	= I conquer, overcome
unda, -ae, f.	= wave

Detective work

nymphās	What is the English equivalent?
vulnerō	Our word vulnerable describes someone who may be wounded.
captō	This verb mean "to chase" rather than "to capture".
plācō	What does placate mean?
excitō	What does excite mean?
lāna	The French nursery rhyme begins *"Baa, baa, brebis noir, as-tu de la **laine**…"*
prŏvocābit/exclāmāvit	Which English verbs are derived from these?
Arachnē	What do you think the zoological term '**arachnid**' means?

More tenses of sum

You have already learnt the present tense of *sum* = 'I am' (see page 2). Before tackling the following passage, you need to work out how the future and imperfect tenses will work. To get you started, *erō* = I shall be and *eram* = I was. After that, once you know that they rhyme with the *-bō, -bis, -bit* and *-bam, -bās, -bat* endings which you already know you won't have too much trouble.

Ceres loses her daughter Proserpina

Cerēs erat dea. agricultūram cūrābat. deae fīlia erat Prŏserpina. fīliam dea 1
amābat et puella deam amābat. amīcās quoque puella amābat. amīcae eam
amābant.

ōlim Prŏserpina et amīcae ambulābant. amīcae violās portābant. deae
fīlia quoque violās portāre volēbat. ēheu Prŏserpina! quod violās portāre 5
volēbās, sōla errāvistī. puella sōla errābat et Plūtō eam spectābat. statim
eam amāvit. quid Plūtō putābat? sīc putābat: puella est fīlia deae. eam
amō. rēx sum. puella rēgīna erit.

ēheu! ubĭ nunc sunt Prŏserpinae amīcae? puella amīcās vocāvit – sed
frūstrā. lacrimāvit et tunicam lacerāvit – sed frūstrā. 10

Questions

1. How is Ceres described in line 1.
2. Who was Proserpina?
3. What were Proserpina's friends doing in line 4?
4. What happened to Proserpina in lines 5–7 when she decided to copy her friends?
5. What did Pluto think when he saw Proserpina in lines 6–7?
6. In the last paragraph, what happened when Proserpina called to her friends?

Vocabulary

ambulō, -āre	= I walk
errō, -āre	= I wander
fīlia, -ae, f.	= daughter
frūstrā	= in vain
ōlim	= once upon a time
putō, -āre	= I think
quid?	= what?
sīc	= thus
viola, -ae, f.	= violet

Detective work

amīca	French *ami*. What does **amicable** mean?
eam	This means her, in the sense of "the boy loves her". Note how the *-am* ending rhymes with the *-am* ending of *puellam* when it is the object.
portābant	If something is portable, it can be carried.
volēbat, volēbās:	from our irregular verb *volō* = I wish.
sōla	Think of sole, solitary, solo etc.
rēx	On post boxes, one often sees the letters GR (*Georgius Rēx*).
tunica	A standard article of Roman dress.
lacerāvit	If something is **lacerated**, what has happened to it?

Ceres searches for her daughter

semper Cerēs lacrimābat. diū errābat et incolās terrae interrogābat. "ubĭ est fīlia?" taedās tandem flammīs Aetnae īnflammāvit et iterum errābat. "ubĭ est fīlia? ubĭ est fīlia?" Prŏserpinam semper vocābat sed frūstrā. dea īrāta erat. incolās Siciliae culpāvit et terram vastāvit. tandem nympha Arethūsa fābulam deae nārrāvit.

"ego, ō Cerēs, Siciliam amō. tū quoque Siciliam amās. patriam amāmus. nunc ego patriam servābō. Prŏserpinam spectāvī. Prŏserpina rēgīna est quod Plūtō eam amat. puella Siciliam amat et semper cūrābit. tū quoque, ōrō, terram Siciliam nōn iam vastābis."

Vocabulary

Arethūsa	= a nymph who was turned into a spring which is still there in present-day Syracuse
culpō, -āre	= I blame
diū	= for a long time
ego, tū	= I, you (pronouns, used for emphasis)
fābulā, -ae, f.	= story
iterum	= again
ōrō, -āre	= I beg
puella, -ae, f.	= girl
taeda, -ae, f.	= pine torch
ubĭ?	= where?

Detective work

interrogābat	We use the word interrogate.
Aetnae	It's still belching flames.
īnflammāvit	Think of the word inflame.
īrāta	How do you feel if you are irate?
vastāvit	Put de- in front and you get which English verb?
patriam	Patriotic people love their ...
servābō	What do we try to do to the environment in a **Conservation** Area?

Proserpina and the pomegranate seeds

As you have read already, while Proserpina was picking flowers in Sicily, suddenly Pluto, god of the Underworld, appeared as if from nowhere in a black chariot with fiery black horses. He fell in love with the young girl and carried her off to be his queen, hurling his sceptre into a pool in order to open up a way down for them.

Ceres was in despair and searched the whole world for her daughter both night and day, but in vain. Eventually, on her return to Sicily, she noticed Proserpina's girdle floating in the pool where Pluto had descended and in a fit of uncontrolled grief, blamed the Sicilians for her loss, breaking their ploughs and sending plague to both farmers and animals.

Fortunately the nymph Arethusa, who like Proserpina had been pursued by a god (and transformed into a fountain) had seen Proserpina when her own stream had carried her underground. She tried to console Ceres and begged her not to destroy Sicily, a land they both loved. When she heard the news Ceres went to Jupiter (the father of her child) and insisted that he intervene. "A plunderer is not a suitable husband for your daughter," she argued. Jupiter reminded her that Pluto was his own brother and that the kidnapping sprang from love, not malice. However, after thinking it over for a while he said that the fates had decreed that Proserpina could return to her mother - provided that she had not eaten anything. Unhappily she had swallowed some pomegranate seeds; it was agreed therefore that she should spend half the year as Queen of the Underworld and the other half with her mother. This myth, as you will probably have realised, explains the seasons. When Ceres was separated from Proserpina, she was sad and the earth was barren; but when she was reunited with her she was happy and the earth became fruitful.

So, when you eat your breakfast **cereal** from now on, spare a thought for Ceres!

Revision

Can you give the names of the following?

1. The three headed dog.
2. The ferryman of the Styx.
3. The man tormented by grapes which kept moving out of his reach.
4. The man who went to the Underworld to bring back his dead wife.
5. The king of the gods.
6. The queen of the gods.
7. The god of the sun.
8. The god of the sea.
9. The goddess of love.
10. The goddess of wisdom.
11. The god of the Underworld.
12. The god of war.
13. The goddess of the moon and hunting.
14. The messenger god.
15. The god of fire.

Chapter 3
Prepositions

Now for some more practice with nouns, and a bit of fun with prepositions. All pretty easy stuff, if you keep your eye on the noun endings, so here we go!

Ubĭ sum?

In the following passages three places are described which were very well-known in ancient times – and still are.

I: Harēna

in harēnā sum et incolae Rōmae mē spectant. subitō ferae intrant et incolās excitant. dum cum ferīs pugnāre parō, incolae clāmant. etiam fēminae clāmant quod mē amant! ferās superābō et fēminae mē laudābunt. ferās iterum superābō et incolae mē servābunt. fortasse, ēheu, ferās nōn superābō et incolae mē damnābunt. lacrimābuntne fēminae? nōn semper! ubĭ sum?

Vocabulary

cum + abl.	=	with
damnō, -āre	=	I condemn
dum	=	while
etiam	=	even
in + abl.	=	in
parō, -āre	=	I prepare
subitō	=	suddenly

Detective work

harēna	Remove the h and there's your word. It means sand in Latin.
fera	The English derivation is **ferocious**, so what sort of animal is this?
excitant	Easy enough to work out.
clāmant	If there is a lot of clamour, what are people doing?
laudābunt	What does laudable mean?

Thumbs up?

Spectators at a gladiatorial show were able to participate in a very dramatic way. If they considered that the gladiators had performed well, they could "vote" for their lives to be spared by either putting their thumbs up or down (no one seems sure which). If they thought they had performed less well, they "voted" for them to be killed. Some gladiators became such favourites with the crowd that they were spared again and again and came back for show after show.

II: Ītalia

in Ītaliā sum. in Viā Sacrā Rōmae cum amīcīs ambulō. ante āram stāmus et flammam spectāmus. puellās quoque spectāmus. flammam puellae cūrant et semper cūrābunt quod Rōmam amant. flamma numquam exstīncta erit. Rōma igitur numquam exstīncta erit. ubĭ sum?

Vocabulary

ante + acc.	=	before, in front of
āra, -ae, f.	=	altar
igitur	=	therefore
stō, stāre,	=	I stand
stetī, statum		
via, -ae, f.	=	road, street

Detective work

exstīncta Vestal Virgins were given the important job in Rome of keeping the flame burning in the Temple of Vesta. Should the flame ever go out, Rome and her empire would fall.

III: Troia

Troiam cum collēgīs oppugnō. cum incolīs Troiae diū pugnāvimus neque dea Fortūna incolās Graeciae amat. nunc igitur hīc sum. vix spīrō propter turbam collēgārum. ēheu, cūr collēgae semper stant ubĭ ego stāre volō? cūr galeās collēgae collocant ubĭ ego galeam collocāre volō? cūr aut hastae aut galeae collēgārum mē semper vexant! ubĭ sum?

Vocabulary

collēga, -ae, m.	=	comrade
collocō, -āre	=	I place
galea, -ae, f.	=	helmet
hasta, -ae, f.	=	spear
neque	=	and not/but not
oppugnō, -āre	=	I attack
propter + acc	=	on account of
turba, -ae, f.	=	crowd
vix	=	scarcely

Detective work

spīrō What does artificial respiration help one to do?

vexant The old-fashioned verb to vex should help.

The not so witless wasp

1 Valeria et Lūcia et Iūnia īn silvīs ambulābant. subitō vespa appropinquāvit.
vespās Valeria nōn amat. quod vespās Valeria nōn amat, vespae semper ad
Valeriam volant. vespa igitur nec Lūciam nec Iūniam vexāvit. Valeriam tamen
saepe vexābat. circum puellam ter volāvit.

5   Valeria clāmāvit sed vespa circum puellam volāvit. Valeria iterum clāmāvit
et īram vespae excitāvit. murmurābat vespa et lacrimābat puella. "ō Iuppiter!"
inquit "cūr vespae hīc habitant? cūr terrās nōn pūrgāvistī? ēheu, ēheu!"

Lūcia quoque lacrimābat quod vespa amīcam perturbābat. "vespam"
inquit "necābō et amīcam servābō." sed Iūnia amīcam castīgāvit (amīcās
10 saepe castīgābat) et ad vespam ambulāvit. "vespās" inquit "Valeria nōn amat.
eam igitur vespae semper vexant. ego vespās amō. ego vespās numquam
necō. mē igitur vespae nec vexant nec perturbant.

vespa ad Iūniam volāvit. puella "vespae" inquit "mē numquam…vae! vae!"
vulnerāvitne Iūniam vespa? fortasse. etiam vespae arrogantiam nōn amant!

Questions

1. What were the three girls doing in line 1 when the wasp appeared?
2. Which of the girls did not like wasps?
3. What did the wasp do in line 4 to annoy Valeria?
4. What were the two questions that Valeria asked Jupiter in line 7?
5. Why was Lucia crying in line 8?
6. What did Lucia plan to do in lines 8–9?
7. Explain why Iunia was confident that the wasp would not sting her?
8. Was she right to be so confident?

Vocabulary

ad + acc.	= towards
ambulō, -āre	= I walk
circum + acc.	= around
inquit	= he/she says
īra, -ae, f.	= anger
tamen	= however
vae	= alas!
vespa, -ae, f.	= a wasp
volō, -āre	= I fly
vulnerō, -āre	= I wound

Detective work

ter	Think of expressions such as ter-centenary.
volāvit	Not to be confused with the irregular verb volō.
murmurābat	People murmur; what do wasps do?
pūrgāvistī	Again, think of which English verb we get from this.
perturbābat	And again!
castīgāvit	And again! (Useful language, Latin!)

Can you escape the rhino?

Life in Rome was never dull. Powerful men and later the emperors regularly put on games, at which a wide range of wild animals would be displayed, often tearing each other to bits, or better still, tearing slaves and Christians to bits. These animals had to be kept somewhere, so imagine the carnage if one escaped...

THE RHINO CHASES YOU – *per viam; ad tabernam; ad īnsulam*; per iānuam in īnsulam.*
ubĭ est fera? vae! iam in īnsulā est; post tē et prope tē est. (ō Iuppiter, cūr in terrā sum? cūr nōn stēlla sum? cūr nōn inter stēllās cum Ursā sum?)
*N.B. as well as meaning an island, this word means a block of flats.

YOU CONTINUE – *per fenestram ex īnsulā; per viam; circum statuās. ubĭ nunc est fera? prope statuās est. (ō Iuppiter, cūr nōn sub terrā sum? cūr nōn sub terram festīnō, ubĭ Prŏserpina mē cūrābit?)*

YOU CONTINUE – *in balneās; inter columnās balneārum et tandem in piscīnam; dum in piscīnā es sub aquā natās.*

Detective work

ad tabernam	Exchange the b for a v to get an old-fashioned English word.
in īnsulam/ in īnsulā	Remember to distinguish between *in* + acc. and *in* + abl.
ursa	i.e. the constellation Ursa Major. What do we call it in English?
fenestra	French **fenêtre**.
sub terrā/ sub terrās	Can you work out why the case after *sub* is sometimes accusative, sometimes ablative?
balneās	These provided a very popular form of leisure activity and also helped people to keep clean…
piscīna	The French word is **la piscine**.

Vocabulary

ē/ex + abl.	= out of
in + acc.	= into
in + abl.	= in
inter + acc.	= between
per + acc.	= through, along
post + acc.	= after, behind
prope + acc.	= near
stēlla, -ae, f.	= star
sub + abl. or acc.	= under

15

CHAPTER 4
2nd conjugation verbs; 2nd declension nouns

King Midas

deus Bacchus vīnum cūrābat. ōlim Sīlēnus satyrus, deī amīcus, īn silvīs errābat. (pōtābat et cantābat et ē viā errāvit.) tandem ad rēgiam errāvit ubī Midās rēx eum ad cibum et vīnum invītāvit.

Bacchus ad rēgiam festīnāvit et "grātiam habeō" inquit "ō rēx, quod amīcum servāvistī. dōnum praebēbō."

Midās "ego quoque" inquit "grātiam habeō, ō Bacche. dōnum mē dēlectābit. aurum mē semper dēlectat et tū aurum praebēre potes. virgam nunc teneō; aurum tenēre volō. pōmum nunc teneō; aurum tenēre volō. aurum habēre semper volō."

ēheu, Midās non satis cōgitāvit!

virgam tenet; statim aurum est. pōmum tenet; statim aurum habet. palmās in aquā lavat; statim aqua aurum est. mēnsās servī ante dominum collocant; cibum rēx tenet; statim cibus aurum est. Midās neque pōtāre neque cēnāre potest quod aqua est solida et cibus est solidus. aurum nōn iam amat!

Vocabulary

aurum, -ī, n.	=	gold
cibus, -ī, m.	=	food
cōgitō, -āre	=	I think
deus, -ī, m.	=	god
dominus, -ī, m.	=	lord, master
dōnum, -ī, n.	=	gift
inquit	=	he/she says
lavō, -āre,	=	I wash
lāvī, lautum (or lavātum)		
praebeō, -ēre	=	I offer
rēgia, -ae, f.	=	palace
satyrus, -ī, m.	=	satyrs were half-goat, half-man creatures, attendants of Bacchus
teneō, -ēre	=	I hold
vīnum, -ī, n.	=	wine
virga, -ae, f.	=	twig

Detective work

eum	If *eam* (feminine) means her, what must *eum* (masculine) mean?
grātiam habeō	Italian **grazie**, Spanish **gracias** and English **grateful**.
dēlectō	Think of delectable.
potes(t)	**pos**sum means I am able and is based closely on the verb *sum*. So what must **potes** and **potest** mean?
satis	If you're **satisfied** you have eaten…?
pōmum	French **pomme.**
palmās	The palms of one's…
solida, solidus	Why do you think these endings are different? (You will learn more about adjectives later.)

16

King Midas (cont.)

Midās subitō perīcula aurī timēbat. ad Bacchum igitur festīnāvit et "peccāvī," 1
inquit. "nunc in perīculō sum; dōnum nōn iam amō. errāvī."

Bacchus "ad fluvium Pactōlum" inquit "ambulāre tē iubeō. aquae fluviī
aurum removēbunt."

rēx statim ad fluvium festīnāvit; digitōs in aquīs lavat; statim aurum ē digitīs 5
Midae in aquās effluit; aqua subitō aurum est!

posteā rēx dīvitiās vītābat; nōn iam in rēgiā sed īn silvīs et in agrīs manēbat.
perīcula dīvitiārum nōn iam ignōrābat!

Questions on King Midas (cont.)

1. What did Midas do in line 1 when he realised how dangerous his gift was?
2. What did Bacchus tell him to do in lines 3–4?
3. Describe what happened when Midas washed his fingers in the water (lines 5–6).
4. How did Midas behave after this episode (lines 7–8)?
5. What is meant by *perīcula dīvitiārum* (line 8)?

Vocabulary

ager, agrī, m.	= field
digitus, -ī, m.	= finger
dīvitiae, -ārum, fem. pl.	= riches
fluvius, -iī, m.	= river
iubeō, -ēre, iussī, iussum	= I order
maneō, -ēre, mānsī, mānsum	= I remain
perīculum, -ī, n.	= danger
posteā	= afterwards
timeō, -ēre, -uī	= I fear
vītō, -āre, -āvī, -ātum	= I avoid

Detective work

errāvī	As well as meaning I wander, *errō* has another meaning from which we get the word error.
effluit	What is an **effluence**?
ignōrābat	If someone does not know something we say they are ignorant.

What do we mean when we say somebody has 'the Midas touch'?

Visit to a Roman town house

The Romans were famous for their building skills. Aqueducts, temples, amphitheatres, huge bath complexes, all can be seen littered across Europe and the Mediterranean world in their wake. But when they had finished conquering huge chunks of the world, or building vast monuments, it was nice to get back home.

Part I

1 *per Iūlium et Augustum Rōmānī saepe ad vīllās rūsticās migrābant. sīc enim morbōs et perīcula Rōmae vītābant. dum autem caelum erat frīgidum, in urbānīs domiciliīs habitābant. sīc domicilia aedificābant.*

*ante domicilium erat **vestibulum** ubĭ ventōs et pluviās Rōmānī vītābant et*
5 *amīcōs salūtābant. per **iānuam** in **ātrium** ambulābant. ōlim ātrium paene tōtum domicilium erat: ibĭ erat **focus**; ibĭ labōrābant; ibĭ cēnam parābant. (Iuppiter! quōmodo spīrāre poterant? quōmodo fūmum vītābant?).*

*in **tēctō** ātriī **compluvium** erat. sub compluviō erat **impluvium**. pluviae per compluvium in impluvium intrābant. erat igitur in ātriō stāgnum! stāgnum*
10 *Rōmānī columnīs ōrnābant. circum ātrium erant **cubicula** ubĭ Rōmānī dormiēbant. per tōtum domicilium fenestrae erant rārae. (Iuppiter! quōmodo vidēre poterant?)*

Vocabulary

autem	= however, moreover
caelum, -ī, n.	= sky, weather
cubiculum, -ī, n.	= bedroom
enim	= for
focus, -ī, m.	= hearth
ibĭ	= there
morbus, -ī, m.	= disease
pluviae	= rains
-ārum, f. pl.	
stāgnum, ī, n.	= pool
tēctum, -ī, n.	= roof
videō, -ēre,	= I see
vīdī, vīsum	

Questions

1. Why did the Romans often leave the city during July and August (lines 1–2)?

2. Explain the function of the following:
   vestibulum (line 4)   *compluvium* (lines 8–9)
   iānua (line 5)   *impluvium* (lines 8–9)
   ātrium (line 5)   *cubicula* (lines 10–11)
   focus (line 6)

Detective work

The following words come from Latin ones used in this passage. Match them up as you go along and you won't need to use the vocabulary:

Rustic; villa; migrate; fri(d)g(e); domicile; urban; vestibule; ventilator; salute; total; fumes; stagnant; column; adorn; cubicle; dormitory; *fenêtre* (French); rare.

domicilia	What is a domicile?
ventōs	**Ventilators** let these in.
paene	A **peninsula** is *paene* an *īnsula*, but not quite.
fūmum	Think of fumes.
poterant	If *potest* = he is able, what tense must *pot**erant*** be and what must it mean?
ōrnābant	Put ad- in front to get the English verb; or think of '**ornament**'.
stagnum	Think of a stagnant pond!
dormiēbant	What do people do in a **dormitory**?

Part II

As Romans grew richer, so their homes became more grand and luxurious.

*ubĭ Rōmānī dīvitiās habēbant, saepe **trīclīnium** aedificābant ubĭ paterfamiliās cum amīcīs cēnābat; saepe enim amīcōs ad convīvium invītābat. in lectīs recumbēbant et auxiliō servōrum ēleganter cēnābant.*

*post domicilium Rōmānī **peristylium** saepe aedificābant; in peristyliō erat **hortus** et in hortō erant columnae; circum peristylium erant cubicula, **bibliothēca**, **balneae**, **culīna**.*

hortōs Rōmānī amābant; in peristyliō igitur nōn in ātriō manēre amābant.

Vocabulary

auxilium, -ī, n.	= help
bibliothēca, -ae, f.	= library
lectus, -ī, m.	= couch
paterfamiliās	= the head of the family
ubĭ	= when (as well as where)

Detective work

recumbēbant	If you are in a **recumbent** posture, what are you doing?
ēleganter	Adverbs in Latin often end in *-ter*. What must this one mean?
convīvium	Attending a party often makes one feel convivial.
hortus	What is horticulture?
culīna	Where are **culinary** skills practised?

Room check

In which room of the house would the following take place? Choose the right room from the following:

in vestibulō; in trīclīniō; in culīnā; in cubiculō; in bibliothēcā; in ātriō; in peristyliō.

1. *servī cibum parābant.*
2. *fēminae prope impluvium sedēbant.*
3. *paterfamiliās studēbat.*
4. *amīcī pluviās vītābant.*
5. *puellae dormiēbant.*
6. *fēminae in hortō prope columnās sedēbant.*
7. *convīvium erat.*

Don't let them swindle you

A farmer owns a PLAUSTRUM (cart) which he uses to carry goods around Rome's seven hills. He charges his customers one *dēnārius* for transporting one item, two *dēnāriī* for transporting more than one. Sometimes he needs extra people to help with transporting the items, in which case the rate doubles. What is the cost of the following journeys?

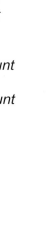

> *agricola mēnsam portāvit*
> *pictūram agricola portāvit*
> *agricola dōna portāvit*
> *galeam portāvit*
> *pōma agricolae portāvērunt*
> *dōna portāvit*
> *feram agricolae portāvērunt*
> *ursam portāvērunt*
> *hastās portāvit*
> *tēlum portāvit*
> *tēla portāvit*
> *tēla portāvērunt.*

Vocabulary

tēlum, -ī, n. = spear

A puzzle

From the information given below fit the correct occupation to each of the five names.
Mārcus, Quīntus, Publius, Gāius, Lūcius sunt amīcī. alius est agricola, alius coquus, alius nauta, alius medicus, alius poēta.

> *neque ventī neque undae Mārcō placent; numquam nāvigat.*
> *Gāius aut terram arat aut cibum parat.*
> *aut Publius aut Mārcus incolās ā perīculō morbōrum servat.*
> *aut Mārcus aut Lūcius trāns undās ad īnsulās nāvigat.*
> *verba Publiō placent; saepe in bibliothēcā sedet.*
> *Quīntus in culīnā labōrat.*

Vocabulary

alius...alius	= one...the other	*medicus, -ī*, m.	= doctor
arō, -āre	= I plough	*placeō, -ēre* (+ dat.)	= I am pleasing (to)
coquus, -ī, m.	= cook	*poēta, -ae*, m.	= poet

CHAPTER 5
Adjectives

Echo and Narcissus

1 *Ēchō erat nympha tenera. Iuppiter nymphās tenerās amābat. Ēchō garrula*
nātūrā erat et semper, dum Iuppiter nymphārum turbam pulchrārum spectābat,
rēgīnam deōrum suspiciōsam multīs verbīs dētinēbat. (sīc enim Iūnō marītum
inter nymphās nōn vidēbat.) ubĭ autem dea cōnsilium nymphae investīgāvit,
5 *īrāta "mē" inquit "lingua tua fraudāvit; linguam igitur tuam dēlēbō; nunc sōlum*
verba aliōrum iterābis."

    ōlim Narcissum, puerum pulchrum et grātum puellīs, dum in agrīs ambulat,
Ēchō vīdit; statim eum amāvit. paene īnsāna erat et quamquam ad locum
appropinquāre volēbat, timida in dēnsā silvā manēbat; sonāre enim prīma
10 *nōn poterat. mox Narcissus amīcōs vocāvit. "quis adest?" inquit et "quis*
adest?" erat nymphae respōnsum.

    attonitus est Narcissus. nēmō adest. iterum vocat. "mē-ne vītās?" iterum
respōnsum nymphae "mē-ne vītās?" est. ubĭ autem puer clāmāvit, "ambulāsne
ad mē?" Ēchō, quod multa ōscula Narcissō dăre volēbat, ē silvā festīnāvit.

Questions

1. Who was Echo (line 1)?
2. How is she described in lines 1–2 and how did she help Jupiter to deceive his wife?
3. How did Juno punish Echo when she discovered that she was being deceived by her (lines 4–6)?
4. Whom did Echo see in lines 7–8 and how is he described?
5. If Echo was keen to meet the boy in lines 8–10, why did she remain hidden in the wood?
6. What was it that the boy did in line 10 which gave Echo the opportunity to speak to him?
7. What was his reaction (line 12)?
8. Why did Echo eventually rush out of the wood (line 14)?

Vocabulary

cōnsilium, -iī, n.	= plan	*pulcher, pulchra,*	= beautiful
dō, dăre,	= I give	*pulchrum*	
dedī, dătum		*quamquam*	= although
grātus, -a, -um	= pleasing	*semper*	= always
iterō, -āre	= I repeat	*sōlum*	= only
locus, -ī, m.	= place	*tener, tenera,*	= tender, young
nēmō	= no one	*tenerum*	
ōsculum, -ī, n.	= kiss	*verbum, -ī*, n.	= word
puer, -ī, m.	= boy		

Detective work

Here are some English words derived from the Latin ones in this passage: suspicious, multiply, detain, irate, reiterate, dense, timid.

garrula	What does garrulous mean?
nātūrā	Notice the final *ā* is long, so what case is it? Which English preposition is needed?
marītum	French ***mari***, English **marital**.
fraudāvit	Fraudulent people are apt to behave this way.
lingua	If you are multi-lingual, you can speak many languages or many…?
tua	*Tuus* means belonging to *tū*.
dēlēbō	The 4th principal part of this verb is *dēlētum*, which gives a good clue to its meaning.
volēbat	You have met the irregular verb *volō* = I wish. Here it is in the imperfect tense.
adest	You have already met the irregular verb *sum*. *Adsum* behaves like *sum* and means I am present.
prīma	If something is of prime quality, into which class do we put it?

Echo is rejected

ēheu! nymphae puer, nec tamen puerō nympha placēbat. Narcissus enim neque amīcōs neque puellās amābat; Narcissus sōlum Narcissum amābat. verba nymphae rīdēbat. "stulta es," inquit. "tē numquam amābō." Narcissus superbus erat! Ēchō misera erat! diū lacrimābat et sub foliīs dēnsīs remōtae silvae sōla iacēbat. mox languida et īnfirma est; tandem nōn iam spīrāvit. mortua est sed vōx nymphae manēbat et per silvās sonābat.

Nemesis autem dea iūstitiam cūrābat nec superbiam hūmānam amābat. Narcissō supplicium aptum dea dedit. fessus enim prope lacum sedēbat. aquās placidās spectābat. subitō puerum pulchrum in aquā vīdit et statim amāvit. nunc tū stultus erās, Narcisse, quod figūram tuam laudāvistī et amāvistī. puer paene īnsānus erat. "tē amō" inquit, "tē amō." nūllum autem respōnsum erat. Narcissus quoque mox languidus et īnfirmus est et quod Narcissum, nōn aliōs, amābat, nōn iam spīrāvit. mortuus prope lacum iacēbat.

subitō folium album ē terrā appāret. mox appārent multa folia alba. amīcī Narcissī nōn iam puerum mortuum sed pulchrum flōrem vident. nōn Narcissus est sed narcissus.

Vocabulary

albus, -a, -um	= white
appāreō, -ēre	= I appear
fessus, -a, -um	= tired
figūra, -ae, f.	= form, shape
folium, -iī, n.	= leaf
iaceō, -ēre	= I lie
mortuus, -a, -um	= dead
neque…neque	= neither…nor
nūllus, -a, -um	= no
rīdeō, rīdēre, rīsī, rīsum	= I laugh (at)
stultus, -a, -um	= stupid
superbus, -a, -um	= proud
supplicium, -iī, n.	= punishment

Detective work

English words to think about: miserable, remote, languid, infirm, placid, insane.

vōx	Our vocal chords control our voice.
iūstitiam	An abstract noun like *arrogantia*. Change the initial i to j and you almost have the English word.
superbiam	Another abstract noun.
prope lacum	Often the meaning of a phrase can be worked out once you have
sedēbat	translated what follows it. Think about where one might find *aquās placidās*.
aptum	We use the word **apt**.
flōrem	What do we buy at a florist's? (You will meet nouns ending in *-em* in the accusative later, when you meet the 3rd declension.)
narcissus	A beautiful flower sprang up in the spot where Narcissus died.

What's going to happen?

Have you ever planned something important and would have liked to know beforehand if it would go well? Would your plan turn out to be a disaster? If so, best to cancel it. Certainly it would sometimes help to be able to foretell the future and that's what the Romans thought. "When men can foretell the future they have the power of the gods" said Cicero, a famous Roman orator and politician.

The Romans used various means to "take the auspices", that is to observe the signs which would indicate whether the gods favoured their plans or not. Of course, if one particularly wanted something to happen, or not to happen, it was quite easy to cheat! Now read about some signs which the Romans said "foretold" their history.

Strange things from the sky

Aeneas, the hero of Virgil's Aeneid, has been told to leave Troy (now that the Greeks in the wooden horse have started to burn it) and to sail across the Mediterranean and found another city. His father Anchises does not wish to leave his homeland but he and Aeneas suddenly see clear signs from the gods.

Graecī ubǐ cum Troiānīs pugnābant Troiam diū obsidēbant neque incolās superāre poterant. cōpiās igitur in equō ligneō cēlāvērunt. sīc tandem malō dolō tōtam Troiam flammīs dēlēvērunt.

Aenēās ubǐ flammās vīdit "Troiam" inquit "Graecī numquam dēlēbunt. quamquam amīcī meī mortuī iacent ego domicilia nostra gladiō meō servābō."

dī autem et deae aliter putābant. Venus sīc eum monuit: "Priamus rēx mortuus iacet. amīcōs tuōs Graecī necāvērunt et fortasse etiam nunc propinquōs tuōs vulnerant. tū sōlus gladiō tuō domicilia servāre numquam poteris. tē trāns aquās cum propinquīs et fīdīs amīcīs nāvigāre iubeō. in aliā terrā aliam patriam habēbis. quod tū et fīlius et amīcī prō patriā vestrā labōrābitis et pugnābitis, nova patria tandem magna et clāra erit."

Aenēās miser erat quod Anchīsēs in patriā suā et in domiciliō suō manēre volēbat. subitō autem dum Ascanium, fīlium Aenēae, spectant (puer enim dormiēbat) spectāculum mīrum vīdērunt. lingua enim flammae, longa sed innoxia, puerī capillōs illūminābat.

Anchīsēs statim "signum" inquit "est deōrum."

> *mox aliud signum vident Aenēās et Anchīsēs. Iuppiter enim in caelō tonat et stēlla per caelum multīs flammīs fulget. Anchīsēs igitur "dī" inquit "multa signa dedērunt. cōnsilium deōrum bonum est. ego quoque trāns aquās nāvigābō. alia Troia in aliā terrā erit."*

This prophecy came true. The "other city" was to be Rome. But Virgil told his story about the founding of Rome when Rome already had a large empire, so he knew the prophecy could not be wrong!

Vocabulary

aliter	= otherwise	*ligneus, -a, -um*	= wooden
capillus, -ī, m.	= hair	*magnus, -a, -um*	= big, great
cēlō, -āre	= I hide	*malus, -a, -um*	= bad
clārus, -a, -um	= famous	*mīrus, -a, -um*	= marvellous
cōpiae,	= forces, troops	*noster,*	= our
-ārum, f. pl.		*nostra, nostrum*	
dolus, -ī, m.	= trickery, deceit	*obsideō, -ēre,*	= I besiege
equus, -ī, m.	= horse	*obsēdī, obsessum*	
fulgeō, -ēre, fūlsī	= I flash, gleam	*signum, -ī,* n.	= sign
gladius, -ī, m.	= sword	*stēlla, -ae,* f.	= star
iubeō, -ēre	= I order	*tonō, -āre, tonuī*	= I thunder

Detective work

dī	Nom. plural of *deus*
propinquī	You know the preposition *prope* = near, so these are your nearest and dearest.
poteris	From *possum*. Think of what *eris* means and that should help.
fīdīs	They show fidelity (like a good Hi-Fi system!)
nova	A novelty is not the same old thing, it's …
vestra	*vester* means belonging to *vōs*.
innoxia	The prefix *in-* makes the word negative, i.e. it is *not* noxious.
spectāculum	Think of spectacular.

A bird behaves strangely

In its early days, when it was still just a small town, Rome was ruled by kings. To the north lived the Etruscans, in the area we now call Tuscany (the Romans called them Tusci as well as Etrusci). An ambitious Etruscan, Tarquin, who had piled up lots of money but was not particularly respected in his home town, one day decided to try his luck in Rome and went to live there with his wife Tanaquil. When they reached the Janiculum, one of Rome's seven hills, a strange incident occurred. Tanaquil interpreted it as a good omen and she was right.

Tanaquil, fēmina Tusca, clāra esse volēbat. saepe igitur marītō Tarquiniō 1
"tē" inquit "quamquam vir strēnuus es et multās dīvitiās habēs, Tuscī numquam
laudant. populus Rōmānus populus novus est. in Etrūriā numquam clārus
esse poterās sed in populō novō fortasse glōriam et fāmam comparāre poteris."

  ex Etrūriā igitur in agrōs Rōmānōs in carpentō migrāvērunt. mox in 5
Iāniculō sedēbant. subitō aquila dē caelō dēvolat et pilleum Tarquiniī rōstrō
āmovet. ubĭ super carpentum ter volāvit, rōstrum laxat et statim pilleus in
locō suō est.

  attonitus est Tarquinius. "aquila" inquit "aut stulta aut īnsāna est."
Tanaquil autem "tū, nōn aquila, stultus es. aquila enim est nūntius deōrum. 10
hīc cum populō Rōmānō habitāre dēbēmus quod dī tē rēgnum spērāre iubent.
rēx Rōmānōrum eris. ego quoque fāmam et glōriam habēbō quod rēgīna
erō. Rōma nunc patria nostra erit."

Tarquin was king in Rome for thirty-eight years. His son, the infamous Tarquin the Proud, was the last king of Rome.

Vocabulary

aquila, -ae, f.	= eagle
carpentum, -ī, n.	= two-wheeled carriage
comparō, -āre	= I win, get
dē (+ abl.)	= down from
pilleus, -ī, m.	= felt cap
populus, -ī, m.	= a people
rēgnum, -ī, n.	= kingdom
rōstrum, -ī, n.	= beak
super + acc.	= above
vir, virī, m.	= man

Detective work

Match these words to the Latin ones as you go along: feminine, strenuous, glory, fame, migrate, relax, astonished.

marītō (line 1)	What case is this? Translate after *inquit*.
agrōs (line 5)	What would be a better word than fields here?
Iāniculō	The Janiculum was one of Rome's seven hills.
dēvolat	*dē* = down from, *volō* = I fly.

Portents galore

In 55 B.C. Julius Caesar crossed to Britain but a combination of our poor weather and woad-painted ancestors rather put him off and it was another ninety years or so before the Romans began to have a firm foothold here. The Britons didn't always want to be ruled by the Romans, especially when the governors were cruel (as was often the case), so it was not surprising that they occasionally revolted. Most famously Boudicca (or Boadicea as she is sometimes called), the widow of the king of the Iceni, led a revolt against the Romans after the death of her husband in 60 A.D. She captured Camulodunum (Colchester), Verulamium (St. Albans) and Londinium (London), all of which still contain plenty of relics to remind us that the Romans settled here. As for portents, strange things happened before the revolt which encouraged the Britons but alarmed the Romans.

1 *Prasutagus, rēx Icēnōrum, post vītam longam et opulentam, ē testāmentō rēgnum et dīvitiās Rōmānīs relīquit. "sīc enim" inquit "prīnceps, quod socius sum populī Rōmānī, cōpiās vel rēgnum meum vastāre vel propinquōs meōs terrēre vetābit."*

5 *Icēnōrum autem agrōs cōpiae, rēgiam servī Rōmānī vastāvērunt. Boudiccam viduam et fīliās, iam captīvās, verberāvērunt. cōpiārum et servōrum superbiam et violentiam Icēnī tolerāre nōn poterant. rēgīna "populō nostrō" inquit "in rēgnō nostrō nōn in prōvinciā Rōmānā habitāre placet. Rōmānī agrōs nostrōs vastāvērunt, nōs igitur oppida Rōmāna dēlēbimus."*

10 *ante bellum multa portenta Icēnōs excitant, Rōmānōs perturbant. Boudicca et amīcae mīrācula per tōtam prōvinciam magnō gaudiō nūntiant: "statua Victōriae" inquiunt "īn forō Camulodūnī prōna iacet. et in cūriā et in theātrō vōx dīra semper ululat. in aestuāriō Tamesis aquae rubrae sunt et plēnae fōrmīs hūmānīs. quid significant portenta? exitium Rōmānōrum*
15 *significant. nōn iam servī erimus."*

Were the women's prophecies correct? In the short-term, yes, as they captured the three main Roman strongholds in the area; but later the Romans brought in reinforcements and Boudicca was defeated and killed herself.

Questions

1. Who was Prasutagus (line 1)?
2. In line 2, what did Prasutagus bequeath to the Romans in his will?
3. Why did he do this (lines 2–4)?
4. In line 5, how did the Romans betray their obligations to Prasutagus and his people?
5. Who was Boudicca and what did she resolve to do (lines 6–9)?
6. What effect did the portents have on (a) the Iceni and (b) the Romans (line 10)?
7. Describe these portents (lines 12–14).
8. Who is speaking in the last line?

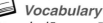

Vocabulary

Camulodūnum, -ī, n.	= Colchester
cūria, -ae, f.	= senate-house
et…et	= both…and
exitium, -iī, n.	= ruin, destruction
gaudium, -iī, n.	= joy
oppidum, -ī, n.	= town
plēnus, -a, -um (+ abl.)	= full
ruber, rubra, rubrum	= red
socius, -iī, m.	= ally
vel…vel	= either…or
verberō, -āre	= I whip
vidua, -ae, f.	= widow
vīta, -ae, f.	= life

Detective work

Here's your English list again. Match these words up to the corresponding Latin ones: opulent, (last will and) testament, captive, violence, tolerate, province, portent, miracle, prone, dire, estuary, form, signify, servile.

prīnceps	An honorary title given to the Roman Emperor.
vastāvērunt (line 5)	Translating this verb is quite tricky, as it has to serve two subjects and two objects. Look at the endings carefully and you should be fine.
nōs	Like the French *nous*, this can be subject or object.
ululat	Say this word again and again aloud and you should get the meaning.
Tamesis	Which river is this?

Poor Cassandra

The god of prophecy was Apollo, who communicated with men through special priests and priestesses. He loved Cassandra, daughter of King Priam, and gave her the gift of prophecy. But Cassandra resisted Apollo's amorous advances, and so he made her pay a terrible price…

Apollō deus fātidicus erat. Cassāndrae, fīliae Priāmī, quod eam amāvit, dōnum dīvīnum dedit. "tū quoque" inquit "per dōnum meum futūrum prōvidēre poteris."

puella igitur Troiānōs saepe monēbat: "Troiānōs Graecī superābunt. Troiam flammīs dēlēbunt. Troiānī rēgnum Ītalicum habēbunt." verba autem Cassāndrae, quamquam vēra erant, Troiānōs nōn mōvērunt. nēmō puellae crēdēbat, quod sīc deus Apollō iussit.

tandem Agamemnōn, rēx Graecōrum, cum Cassāndrā captīvā ad Graeciam victor nāvigāvit. ibǐ Clytaemnēstra rēgīna marītum in rēgiā multō gaudiō, multā pompā exspectābat. puella autem Troiāna statim futūrum dīvīnāvit. "rēgīna" inquit "tē, quod fīliam Īphigenīan dīs sacrificāvistī, nōn iam amat. gaudium simulat sed nōs necābit."

Agamemnōn rēx Cassandrae nōn crēdēbat. verba autem puellae vēra erant. Clytaemnēstra enim et marītum et puellam Troiānam necāvit.

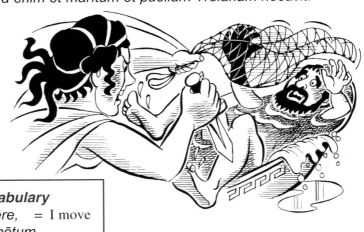

Vocabulary

moveō, -ēre, = I move
    mōvī, mōtum
prōvideō, -ēre = I foresee
vērus, -a, -um = true

Detective work

fātidicus	Literally "telling the fates".
crēdēbat	This verb is followed by the dative. We get the word credible and, of course, incredible.
Clytaemnēstra	The usual English spelling is Clytemnestra.
Īphigenīan	This is an example of a Greek accusative. After all, Iphigenia was Greek!
dīs	Dative plural of *deus*.
simulat	We use the word simulate.

Consulting the oracle

There were several oracles in the ancient world but the most famous one was at Delphi, in northern Greece. The early Greeks consulted it frequently as it had a great reputation and they received their answers from priests and priestesses who had been "inspired" (*in + spīrō* – useful language, Latin!) by the god until they were in a dream-like state. Sometimes (perhaps to impress) they threw their arms about as if in a frenzy. The answers given could often be somewhat ambiguous. This was particularly the case when the priests wrote their answer on leaves which they then flung to the winds. If one wanted to discover the answer, one had to scrabble about among the leaves and do some jig-saw work, piecing the words together into a sentence.

Here are some "oracular answers" for you to piece together. You have to be quite slick at matching adjectives to nouns, of course, but after all the practice you've had you'll soon be as quick as the Romans at getting the right answer. In some cases, for greater authenticity, more than one answer is possible!

Answer to Tantalus

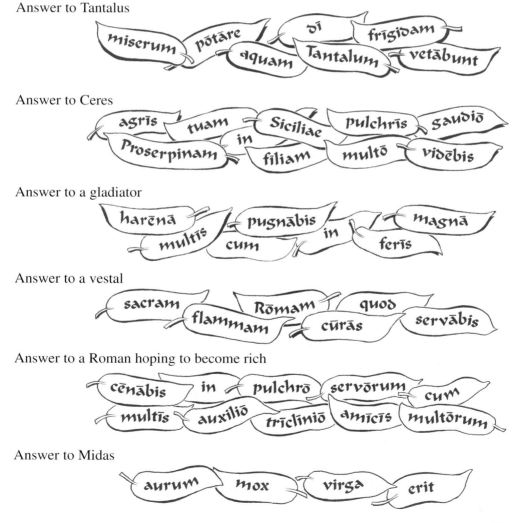

Answer to Ceres

Answer to a gladiator

Answer to a vestal

Answer to a Roman hoping to become rich

Answer to Midas

CHAPTER 6
3rd and 4th conjugation verbs

King Midas never learns

(Continuing the bizarre story of Midas)

ōlim deus Pān turbae nymphārum īn silvīs cantābat. Midās, quod īn silvīs nōn in rēgiā iam habitābat, saepe deum audiēbat. eum semper laudābat. "ō Pān," inquit "quam bene cantās."

verba Midae Phoebō nōn placēbant. Phoebus enim deus mūsicōrum erat. laurō corōnātus lyram sinistrā, plēctrum dextrā tenuit. quam bene cantābās, Phoebe! Midās autem aliter putābat. "Pān" inquit "nōn Phoebus mē dēlectat."

īrātus erat deus mūsicōrum. "aurēs" inquit "Midae hūmānam fōrmam nōn retinēbunt. asinus enim est. aurēs igitur asinī habēbit."

mox Midās murmura et susurrōs circum aurēs sēnsit. aurēs et sinistrā et dextrā tangit. vae! longae et hirsūtae sunt! tandem aurēs asinī cēlāre nōn iam potest. quis eum adiuvābit? nēmō. sociī eum rīdēbunt.

Vocabulary

asinus, -ī, m.	= ass
dextra, -ae, f.	= right hand
quam bene	= how well
mūsicus, -ī, m.	= musician
retineō, -ēre	= I retain
sinistra, -ae, f.	= left hand
socius , -ī, m.	= companion
tangō, -ere, tetigī, tāctum	= I touch

Detective work

laurō	A tree sacred to Phoebus Apollo. He wore a wreath of this on his head.
corōnātus	When a king or queen is crowned, what do we call the ceremony?
lyram	A lyre is a stringed instrument.
plēctrum	We still use this word, e.g. when playing a guitar.
aurēs	In an aural examination, the ears are used (you will be meeting more of these 3rd declension endings soon. For now, note that -ēs can be both nominative and accusative plural.)
susurrōs	Say the word aloud a few times. What sort of sound is it?
hirsūtae	Hirsute men are very hairy.

King Midas' secret is revealed

rēx igitur, quod aurēs cēlāre volēbat, magnam tiāram semper gerēbat. diū
rīsum amīcōrum vītābat. sed forte servus, dum Midae capillōs et barbam
cūrat, aurēs asinī sub tiārā vīdit. "dominum meum" inquit "prōdere nōn dēbeō.
sed fābula mīra est. tacēre nōn possum."

terram igitur excavat et fābulam terrae recitat. "fābulam" inquit " nōn 5
dīvulgāvī. eam enim sub terrā cēlāvī."

mox autem herbae et calamī nōn sōlum ē terrā surgunt sed etiam in
ventīs murmurant et susurrant. tōtam igitur fābulam ē terrā revocant et sociīs
Midae dīvulgant.

Vocabulary

calamus, -ī, m.	= reed
forte	= by chance
gerō, -ere	= I wear
herba, -ae, f.	= grass
prōdō, -ere	= I betray
surgō, -ere	= I rise
taceō, -ēre	= I keep silent

Questions

1. Why did Midas always wear something on his head (line 1)?
2. Who was the first to discover Midas' secret (lines 2–3)?
3. Why was this person reluctant to tell anyone else what he had seen (line 3)?
4. What did he do when he was unable to keep his secret to himself any longer (line 5)?
5. How did the secret get out in the end (lines 7–9)?

Detective work

tiāram	Our word tiara is not quite right here. Choose more suitable headgear!
rīsum	The noun from *rīdeō*.
barbam	A barber trims it (if you have one).
excavat	Think of excavation.
recitat	Think of recite.
eam enim sub terrā cēlāvī (line 6)	The *eam* refers to the story, and should be translated as "it" (in Latin *eam* really means "her", because *fābula* is feminine.)
revocant	*Re* means back or again.

Roman clothes

What will Marcus wear?

nōs: *quid hodiē geris, Mārce?*

Mārcus: *hodiē **tunicam** gerō.*

nōs: *quid crās gerēs, Mārce?*

Mārcus: *crās tunicam geram. semper tunicam gerō. propinquī meī quoque tunicam gerent. amīcī meī tunicam gerent…*

nōs: *grātiās agimus, Mārce. verba tua audīvimus et intellēximus. nōnne Iūlia et Flāvia quoque tunicās gerent?*

Mārcus: *vae! Iūlia et Flāvia **stolās** gerent. stola est tunica longa; stola modestiam fēminārum cūrat et…*

nōs: *grātiās agimus, Mārce; stultī nōn sumus.*

Mārcus: *tunicam saepe gerō dum dormiō; propinquī meī tunicam gerunt dum dormiunt; amīcī meī tunicās gerunt dum dormiunt; Rōmānī semper…*

nōs: *satis est, Mārce. intellēximus. quōmodo lavās tunicam?*

Mārcus: *famulī (servī domesticī) tunicās et stolās et vestīmenta lavant. dum caelum frīgidum est multās tunicās saepe gerō. avunculus meus…*

nōs: *intellegimus. avunculus tuus quoque multās tunicās gerit…*

Mārcus: *stultī estis. avunculus vir nōtus est. in viīs et īn forō et in cūriā avunculus **togam** gerit. toga est textum longum. umerōs avunculī meī togā servī magnā cūrā involvunt. herī avunculus īrātus famulōs (et mē!) terruit. ē lectō sērō surrēxit. multōrum famulōrum auxiliō domō sērō discessit. sērō ad cūriam advēnit.*

nōs: *cūr nōn cucurrit?*

Mārcus: *stultī estis. avunculus meus togam gerēbat. dum togam gerit numquam currit, numquam cucurrit, numquam curret. vestīmentum est augustum.*

nōs: *sī Flāvia, dum togam gerit…*

Mārcus: *quid dīcis? fēminae togam nōn gerunt. sōlum virī Rōmānī togam gerunt. sī caelum est frīgidum fēminae umerōs **pallā** involvunt.*

nōs:	*num virī, dum pluit, togam augustam gerunt? dum pluit, quid avunculus tuus gerit? quōmodo ventōs et pluviās vītat?*
Mārcus:	**lacernam** *gerit, sed suprā togam nōn īnfrā. neque Rōmānī lacernam īn forō gerunt. Cicerō Mārcum Antōnium castīgāvit quod lacernam nōn togam īn forō gessit.*
nōs:	*Cicerō ōrātor notus erat. saepe īn forō multā sapientiā dīcēbat. Mārcus Antōnius Cleopatram amābat et….*
Marcus:	*grātiās agō. satis est. verba vestra audīvī et intellēxī.*

Vocabulary

augustus, -a, -um	= venerable, majestic	*īnfrā* + acc	= beneath
auxilium, -iī, n.	= help	*intellegō, -ere,*	= I understand
crās	= tomorrow	*-ēxī, -ēctum*	
cūria, -ae, f.	= senate house	*involvō, -ere*	= I wind around
currō, -ere,	= I run	*lectus, -ī,* m.	= bed
cucurrī, cursum		*pluit*	= it rains
grātiās agō	= I give thanks	*sērō*	= late
herī	= yesterday	*suprā*	= over
hodiē	= today	*umerus, -ī,* m.	= shoulder

Detective work

avunculus	We use the word avuncular to describe our uncles.
vestīmenta	French *vêtements*.
textum	English *textiles* is derived from this.
surrēxit	The supine of this verb is *surrēctum*. At the resurrection, Christ rose again (*re + surgō*)

N.B. Roman boys below the age of sixteen, and senior magistrates and priests, wore a toga with a purple band around its border. All other males wore a plain white toga. Try to remember this, you will need it later.

Girls can fly

1 *Mārcus cum Iūliā et Flāviā in hortō sedēbat. subitō Flāvia "puer" inquit "esse volō. puerī tunicās, puellae stolās gerunt. puellae igitur aut in ātriō aut in peristyliō occupātae sedent et lānam dūcunt. neque celeriter currere neque in Campō Mārtiō lūdere possunt. vestīmenta enim longa eās semper*
5 *impediunt."*

rīsit Mārcus. "puellās" inquit "nōn vestīmenta sed nātūra puellārum impedit. puellae perīcula timent. lānae cūram et deam Minervam nātūrā amant. puellae numquam celeriter currunt, numquam tēla mittunt quod timidae sunt. puellae numquam..."

10 *Iūlia "satis est" inquit. "puellae tēla nōn mittunt quod puellae in tēlīs per caelum volant."*

Mārcus iterum rīsit. "quid dīcis? īnsāna es. quōmodo puellae volāre possunt?"

Iūlia "puerī" inquit "poētās nostrōs nōn legunt. fābulam nōtam nārrābō."

Vocabulary

dīcō, -ere, dīxī, dictum	= I say
esse	= to be
lūdō, -ere, lūsī, lūsum	= I play
mittō, -ere, mīsī, missum	= I send, throw (a weapon)
sedeō, -ēre, sēdī, sessum	= I sit
tēlum, -ī, n.	= weapon

Detective work

lānam dūcunt	What activity involves "leading wool" into a thin thread?
celeriter	If you accelerate, the car travels more...
eās	Them (feminine of *eōs*)
Campus Mārtius	The Plain of Mars, where young Roman males exercised.
nātūrā amant (line 7–8)	Take care with this. Why can't *nātūrā* be the subject?
volant	Not from our irregular verb *volō* = I wish, but from *volō, -āre* = I fly.

Iulia's story of Camilla

1 *rēx nōtus Volscōrum propter superbiam īram populī excitābat. tandem, quod poenam timēbat, ē rēgnō cum parvā fīliā Camillā fūgit.*

puellam parvam amābat et fessam saepe in umerīs portābat. dum per agrōs et silvās errant subitō fluvium aquīs rapidīs vīdit. "ēheu!" inquit, "Camilla
5 *natāre nōn potest. quōmodo eam ad alteram rīpam mittere poterō? aquās fīlia parva timēbit sed Volscī mē ad rēgnum redūcere et pūnīre volunt. fortasse dī nōs adiuvābunt."*

36

diū dēlīberābat. tandem fīliam hastae et longae et solidae magnā cūrā
ligāvit. sonant aquae. lacrimat puella. haesitat rēx. hastane īn fluvium cadet?
aquaene fīliam oppriment?

tandem hastam dextrā tenuit et trepidus trāns aquās violentās mīsit.
ecce! tēlum in alterā rīpā fīxum est! Camilla salva est! rēx statim per aquās
rapidās natāvit et fīliae multa ōscula dedit.

Camilla adulta perīcula numquam timēbat. nōn lānam et Minervam sed
equōs amābat. quamquam fēmina erat, patriam dēfendēbat. et virōs et equōs
in proelium dūxit. Camilla sīcut ventī, nōn sīcut puerī stultī, currēbat. ego
nōn puer sed Camilla esse volō.

Vocabulary

alter, altera, alterum	= other (of two)
cadō, -ere, cecidī, cāsum	= I fall
poena, -ae, f.	= punishment
ligō, -āre	= I bind, tie
opprimō, -ere, oppressī, oppressum	= I overwhelm
rīpa, -ae, f.	= river-bank
salvus, -a, -um	= safe
sīcut	= just as
proelium, -ī, n.	= battle

Detective work

Helpful English list: alternative, punish, to deliberate, hesitate, trepidation (and intrepid), fixed, patriotic.

Questions

1. Why was the king of the Volsci unpopular with his people (line 1)?
2. What did he eventually do to escape retribution (lines 1–2)?
3. Who was Camilla (line 2)?
4. Why was the king troubled when he came to the river (lines 4–5)?
5. Why was it so essential that he and Camilla cross the river (lines 5–6)?
6. Describe how the king managed to get Camilla across the river (lines 8–12).

Chapter 7
Roman numerals; *fīlius, deus* and *vir*

Niobe pushes her luck

deus Phoebus erat fīlius Lātōnae. dea Dĭāna erat fīlia Lātōnae. ōlim dum deōs virī et fēminae colunt, Niobē, rēgīna Thēbānōrum, incolās Thēbārum Lātōnam colere vetuit.

"cūr" inquit "Lātōnam colitis? ego fīlia sum Tantalī quī cum dīs et deābus cēnābat. alter avus est Atlas (quī caelum umerīs sustinet), alter avus est magnus Iuppiter. ego dīvitiās magnās habeō. ego fōrmam deae habeō. praetereā ego septem fīliōs et septem fīliās habeō. rēgīnae vestrae dī quattuordecim līberōs pulchrōs, Lātōnae sōlum duōs dedērunt. dea Fortūna mē semper adiuvābit. (stulta erās, Niobē. superbia dīs et deābus nūllō modō placet.)

Lātōna, ubĭ verba rēgīnae audīvit, īrāta erat. "tū Phoebe," inquit, "deus sagittārius es. nōnne verba rēgīnae audīvistī? nōnne mē adiuvābis? num mē, deam Lātōnam, neglegēs? sagittās tuās iam tenēs. tē igitur ad terram mittam."

Phoebus verba Lātōnae intellēxit; sagittās cēpit et ad campum, ubĭ septem fīliōs rēgīnae superbae vīdit, celeriter dēscendit.

Vocabulary

avus, -ī, m.	= grandfather	*nūllō modō*	= in no way
colō, -ere, coluī, cultum	= I worship, cultivate	*praetereā*	= besides
fōrma, -ae, f.	= form, beauty	*quī*	= who, which
līberī, -ōrum, m. pl.	= offspring, children	*sustineō, -ēre*	= I support

Detective work

alter…alter	If you have two alternatives, you can do one thing or the other.
neglegēs	The principal parts are *neglegō, -ere, neglēxī, neglēctum*; so you can work out what this means.
campum	What is a University campus? Do not confuse *campus* with the word for 'camp'.

Niobe pays the price

1 dum septem fīlī rēgīnae equōs trāns campum dūcunt et redūcunt, subitō ūnus ex eīs sonum sagittae audīvit. statim sagittā trānsfīxus cecidit. mox cecidērunt duo, trēs fīlī, deinde quārtus, quīntus, sextus, septimus, omnēs sagittīs trānsfīxī.

Niobē ubĭ fīliōs mortuōs vīdit "ego" inquit "etiam nunc Lātōnam superō;
5 fīlī mortuī sunt sed septem fīliās pulchrās habeō. victōria est mea, Lātōna."

septem fīliae prope sepulchra stābant; puerōs lūgēbant. subitō ūna ē

puellīs sonum sagittae, sīcut frāter, audīvit et statim super sepulchrum mortua 7
cecidit. tum secunda cecidit; tertia, quārta, quīnta, sexta fugiunt sed frūstrā:
mox mortuae sunt. māter, ubǐ sex fīliās mortuās vīdit, "ō Lātōna," inquit "omnēs
fīliōs et sex fīliās necāvistī. nōnne ūnam fīliam servābis? num puellam parvam 10
necābis? – sed frūstrā. cecidit septima quoque.

posteā Niobē semper lacrimat. mox rigida est et tandem figūram statuae
habet sed, ēheu, in aeternum hūmida lacrimīs est. rēgīna superba et stulta
nec tamen mala erat; īra autem deōrum et deārum est dīra.

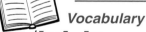

Vocabulary

lūgeō, -ēre,	= I mourn
lūxī, lūctum	
sepulchrum, -ī, n.	= tomb

Detective work

ūnus ex eīs (line 1)	In English we say 'one of them'. In Latin, as you can tell from the fact that *eīs* is coming after *ex* + abl., this must have been "one out of them".
trānsfīxus	What does transfixed mean?
omnēs	All (you will meet more adjectives like this later).
frāter	We get the word fraternal from this.
māter	We get the word maternal from this.
in aeternum	Our phrase is "in eternity".
dīra	What does 'dire' mean in English?

Ancient medicine

Despite her foolish pride you might feel sorry for Niobe. But it was even worse for her children; when Apollo aimed arrows at people, they had no chance of survival!

This of course is all mythological. But what happened in real life? Would you survive a wound from an arrow, or a fever? What if you ate a dish of poisoned mushrooms?

Well, there were doctors (*medicī*) in Ancient Rome, but not many in the early days, and they were not professionally trained or qualified. They were rarely summoned, most households believing that their own knowledge and application of herbal recipes was just as effective as a doctor's treatment, if not better. Later, Greek doctors came to Rome who treated wounded soldiers and gladiators at public expense. However, not all private individuals liked them.

The magic herb

medicōrum antīquōrum aliī iūstī et probī, aliī falsī et fraudulentī erant. Rōmānī igitur medicum ad aegrōs minimē saepe vocābant. sīc enim putābant: avī nostrī scientiam herbārum trādidērunt. nōs igitur aegrōs herbīs et foliīs et unguentīs sānāre possumus.

herba mīra erat lāserpīcium. fēminaene languidae sunt? herba eās stimulābit. puellaene in lectō īnfirmae et miserae iacent? morbum herba dēpellet. ceciditne famulus? tībiamne frēgit? paterfamiliās eum lāserpīciō cūrābit. gemuntne puerī? (ēheu, pōma nōn mātūra ēdērunt!) quōmodo paterfamiliās eōs sānābit? lāserpīciō!

Vocabulary

aeger, aegra, aegrum	=	sick
aliī…aliī	=	some…others
frangō, -ere, frēgī, frāctum	=	I break
gemō, -ere, gemuī, gemitum	=	I groan
lāserpīcium, -iī, n.	=	the plant silphium
probus, -a, -um	=	honest, upright
sānō, -āre	=	I cure
trādō, -ere, trādidī, trāditum	=	I hand over

Detective work

English derivations to help you: antique, false, fraudulent, science, unguent (ointment), languid, stimulate, edible.

minimē saepe
If *minimē* means very little, and *saepe* means often, what must *minimē saepe* mean?

mātūra We get the word mature, but what would be a better word to describe fruit?

tībiam A long thin bone in the leg (it also means a flute!).

Cold hands

ubĭ Rōmānī Graeciam superāvērunt, medicī Graecī ad Ītaliam vēnērunt. quod nōn sōlum aegrōs cūrābant sed etiam medicīnam docēbant, omnēs discipulōs in domicilia aegrōrum saepe invītābant.

Mārtiālis poēta medicum sīc accūsāvit: "languidus eram. tū, ō medice, ad mē cum centum discipulīs vēnistī. centum dextrae frīgidae mē tetigērunt. anteā morbum nōn habuī. nunc habeō."

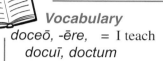

Vocabulary
doceō, -ēre, = I teach
docuī, doctum

Detective work
discipulōs Jesus's disciples were his pupils.

Making a pilgrimage

If the herbal treatment didn't work, or as an extra precaution, the Romans sometimes resorted to spells and superstitious rites. When the poet Tibullus's girlfriend had a bad fever, he spread sulphur round her bed and organised an old crone to chant some spells. Then he tried to calm her delirium three times (a magic number) with consecrated flour and finally made offerings to the goddess Diana nine times at dead of night. She survived – but went off with somebody else!

Some people made a pilgrimage to the temple of Aesculapius, god of medicine, which the Romans had built on an island in the Tiber.

Rōmānī propter pestilentiam dīram templum Aesculāpiī aedificāvērunt, ubĭ deum colēbant. templum saepe aegrīs plēnum erat quī remedium ibĭ petēbant.

deus remedia aegrīs per somnia in tenebrīs nūntiābat. serpentēs quoque in templō erant quī remedium sīc praebēbant: aeger in templō tranquillus iacuit. mox appropinquāvērunt serpentēs quī linguās suprā eum vibrābant. aeger immōtus et serēnus diū manēbat. tandem serpentēs eum linguīs lambēbant. aegrī nūllō modō timēbant neque ūllam iniūriam accipiēbant. salvī et validī erant!

Detective work
Helpful English list: pestilence, remedy, serpent, tranquil, vibrate, serene, injury.

validī If our word invalid comes from *invalidus*, what must *validus* mean?

Vocabulary
accipiō, -ere, = I receive, welcome
accēpī, acceptum
aedificō, -āre = I build
lambō, -ere, = I lick
lambī, lambitum
petō, -ere, = I seek
petīvī, petītum
quī = who
somnium, -iī, n. = dream
ūllus, -a, -um = any

Plaustra not plaustrum

Do you remember when you were a Roman farmer and you had just *ūnum plaustrum* for carting goods around Rome? Soon you had *duo plaustra*, then *tria plaustra*, then you bought *octo* more and now you have *ūndecim plaustra*. Well, now your business has expanded there is of course increasing opportunity for people to swindle you; so check that the payments are correct.

Your customer is speaking –

First load *novem mēnsae et duodēvīgintī gladiī. quīnque et vīgintī in tōtum. pecūniam statim numerābō.*

Second load *quīnquāgintā togae et quadrāgintā lacernae. octōgintā vestīmenta in tōtum. pecūniam statim numerābō.*

Third load *septendecim porcī et duodecim asinī. Iuppiter! quid accidit? equī plaustrum nōn trahent. ubĭ est flagellum? animālia misera et īnfirma sunt. plaustrum trahere nōn possunt. asinōs removēbō. nunc sunt sōlum duodecim porcī. crās pecūniam solvam.*

Fourth load *trecentī narcissī, pulchrī et tenerī. mīlle pōma. duo mīlia olīvārum. trīgintā saccī prūnōrum. summam nunc facere nōn possum. ad cēnam crās ad mē venīre dēbēs. vīnum bibēmus et post cēnam summam faciēmus.*

Vocabulary
bibō, -ere, bibī = I drink
flagellum, -ī, n. = whip
porcus, -ī, m. = pig
prūnum, -ī, n. = plum
trahō, -ere, = I drag
  trāxī, tractum

Detective work

accidit An **accident** means simply something that HAPPENS.

solvam If you are **solvent**, you have … all your debts.

crās If you pro**cras**tinate you put off until … what you should do today.

mīlle pōma/ duo mīlia olīvārum

The Latin adjective meaning one thousand (*mīlle*) is only used to refer to *one* thousand. When referring to two or more thousands, the Romans used the plural noun *mīlia*, which is followed by the genitive case.

CHAPTER 8
3rd declension nouns

Phaethon makes a request

Phaethōn amīcīs saepe "pater meus" inquit "patribus vestrīs nōn similis est. pater meus est Phoebus Apollō, deus sōl."

 ōlim puer, quod amīcī rīdēbant, mātrem dē patre interrogāvit. "māter," inquit "num verba tua falsa sunt? nōnne vēra mihĭ dīxistī?"

 māter "quod mātrī" inquit "nōn crēdis, tē ad rēgiam patris prōcēdere iubeō. Apollō ipse mea verba cōnfirmābit."

 mox Phaethōn ad rēgiam aurō nitidam advēnit, ubĭ sedēbat deus sōl. circum eum dextrā Hōra, Diēs, Mēnsis, Annus, sinistrā Vēr, Aestās, Autumnus, Hiems stābant. ubĭ deus, vestibus aureīs indūtus, surrēxit, puer vix vidēre poterat. oculī enim lūcem splendidam nōn tolerābant. statim Apollō adulēscentem appropinquāre iussit et "māter tua" inquit "vēra dīxit. fīlius Sōlis es. dōnum splendidum tibĭ dabō. quid cupis, mī fīlī?"

 respondit puer: "currum tuum et equōs tuōs quī cotīdiē trāns caelum currunt regere cupiō." palluit Apollō. adulēscentis enim cōnsilium imprūdēns erat. "difficile est" inquit "equōs meōs regere. opus deōrum nōn mortālium est. Iuppiter ipse opus timet. aliud dōnum tibĭ dabō."

 Phaethōn "tū, pater," inquit "prōmīsistī. currum tuum et equōs tuōs trāns caelum regere cupiō." (mēns adulēscentium obstināta semper erat et semper erit.)

Vocabulary

cotīdiē	= every day	mēns, mentis, f.	= mind
currus, -ūs, m.	= chariot (a 4th declension noun – don't worry!)	nitidus, -a, -um	= shining
		opus, operis, n.	= work
		palleō, -ēre	= I am pale
indūtus, -a, -um	= clothed	tibĭ	= to you (dative sing. of tū)
ipse, ipsa, ipsum	= himself, herself, itself		
lūx, lūcis, f.	= light	vēr, vēris, n.	= spring

Detective work

Some of the words in the previous passage may be unfamiliar to you, but think of the following English words and you should be able to work out their meaning: similar; solar; interrogate; credible; annual; pale; mortal, adolescent, imprudent; difficult.

Hōra, Diēs, Mēnsis, Annus

Time is here represented by Hour, Day, Month and Year.

Vēr, Aestās, Autumnus, Hiems

These are the four seasons. *Autumnus* is obvious. "Vernal" and "hibernate" help with two of the others, leaving only *Aestās* (some animals prefer to aestivate than to hibernate).

mī fīlī   Vocative singular.

Phaethon takes a ride

1 *invītus Apollō fīlium ad currum nitidum, opus Vulcānī, ēdūxit. subitō Aurōra portās roseās aperit et dum deus fīlium dē perīculīs monet equī caelum hinnītibus complent. mox per regiōnēs vastās caelī currunt. quod dominus abest ā viā errant; Phaethōn enim eōs retinēre nōn potest.*

5 *paene īnsānī sunt. nunc ascendunt: Ursam Maiōrem et Minōrem terrent. nunc dēscendunt: Lūna, ubĭ frātris equōs videt, attonita est. iterum equī dēscendunt et terram incendunt; flammae ē silvīs, ex arboribus, ē montibus, ex urbibus surgunt. flūmen Nīlus perīculum timet: fugit et caput cēlat.*

tandem Iuppiter, pater omnipotēns, ubĭ vastātiōnem vīdit, "mox Rhēnus"
10 *inquit "et Rhodanus et Padus nōn iam aquās habēbunt. etiam undae, Neptūnī agrī, siccī erunt. multōs hominēs, nōn ūnum adulēscentem, servāre dēbeō." fulmen mīsit et currum frēgit!*

ō miserum Phaethontem! ad terram mortuus cecidistī. pater tuus ubĭ tē mortuum vīdit ūnum tōtum diem tē lūgēbat. ūnum tōtum diem caput manibus
15 *cēlābat. nūllam lūcem hominibus dabat quī "sōlem" inquiunt "nōs miserī numquam iterum vidēbimus."*

Now you know all about the first eclipse!

Vocabulary

arbor, arboris, f.	= tree	*invītus, -a, -um*	= unwilling
Aurōra	= the Goddess of the Dawn	*mōns, montis*, m.	= mountain
		roseus, -a, -um	= rose-coloured
compleō, -ēre, -ēvī, -ētum	= I fill	*siccus, -a, -um*	= dry
		urbs, urbis, f.	= city
fulmen, -inis, n.	= thunderbolt		

Detective work

Link these English words with the appropriate Latin words – aperture, omnipotent; devastation; manual; lucid and translucent.

Nīlus caput cēlat – Who knows who found it again at the end of the nineteenth century?

Now try your hand at some onomatopoeia guesswork (words which sound like their meaning): *hinnītibus*; Horses are around so what is *hinnītus*?

abest *Absum* = I am absent.

Ursam Maiōrem et Minōrem For those of you who don't know your constellations, these are the Greater Bear and the Smaller Bear.

incendunt Think of what an incendiary device does.

Rhēnus, Rhodanus, Padus – they must all be important rivers. Two of them begin Rh… And isn't there a town called Padua which must be situated near the Padus?

hominēs The human race belongs to the species *homŏ sapiēns*.

Questions

1. How enthusiastic was Apollo as he led out his chariot in line 1?
2. What time of day was it when the horses appeared (lines 1–3)?
3. Why did the horses leave their normal route in line 4?
4. Describe what happened as the horses raced through the sky (lines 5–8).
5. Why did Jupiter decide to fire a thunderbolt at the chariot (lines 9–12)?
6. How did Apollo react to this (lines 13–14)?
7. For how long was the world dark (lines 14–15)?
8. What did the men on earth say when the earth went dark (lines 15–16)?

Roman Hospitality

In an age when there were no hotels or campsites, the Romans regarded it as a moral duty to offer accommodation for the night to anyone who knocked at the door. Similarly, a guest would never harm his host or his property. So strict was this code, indeed, that the Latin word for guest and host was the same: *hospes*. The following myth illustrates how seriously the gods regarded any breaking of the rules of hospitality.

Philemon and Baucis – a hospitable old couple

ōlim Iuppiter, rēx deōrum, cum Mercuriō, nūntiō deōrum, ā monte Olympō ad terram dēscendit. duo caelicolae hospitium et cibum ā mortālibus petēbant, sed frūstrā. nēmō eōs accēpit. tandem Philēmōn et Baucis, quī sōlī in parvā casā habitābant, deōs ad cēnam invītāvērunt.

nec dīvitiās nec famulōs habēbant duo rūsticī. quamquam seniōrēs erant, Baucis ipsa marītī auxiliō cibum parāvit. "hospitēs" inquit "sumus. cēnam bonam parāre dēbēmus."

in culīnā dīligenter labōrābat et marītum mēnsam ōrnāre iussit. tandem cibum nōn sūmptuōsum sed bonum hospitibus praebuit. dum omnēs olīvās, ōva, nucēs edunt, vīnum, quamquam Philēmōn pōcula hospitum saepe complēbat, numquam dēficiēbat. attonitī sunt rūsticī.

Vocabulary

casa, -ae, f.	= cottage
crēscō, -ere,	= I grow
crēvī, crētum	
hospitium, -iī, n.	= hospitality
hospes, hospitis, m.	= host or guest
nux, nucis, f.	= nut
ōvum, -ī, n.	= egg
pōculum, -ī, n.	= cup, goblet

Detective work

Useful English derivations: senior citizens, diligent, sumptuous, deficient.

caelicolae	*incolae* of the *caelum*!
dīligenter	Many adverbs in Latin end in *-ter*.

The gods show their gratitude

1 *Philēmōn perturbātus uxōrī "nōnne dolus est?" inquit. Baucis autem āstūta marītō "dī sunt" inquit. "cibus noster dīs nōn placet. convīvium splendidum spērābant. age! nōs pūnient! age! fulmen mox mittent!" et marītum ānserem, quī parvam casam custōdiēbat, necāre iussit. dī autem vetant. "cēna vestra"*
5 *inquiunt "dīs apta est quod magnō gaudiō et magnā līberālitāte eam praebuistis.*

sōlī vōs hospitium dīs dedistis. vīcīnōs igitur omnēs pūniēmus. vōs casam
relinquere et montem ascendere iubēmus. poena enim incolārum dīra erit."

    duo rūsticī casam relīquērunt et ubĭ ad summum montem vēnērunt trepidī
respexērunt. tōtam regiōnem aquīs submersam vident. ūnum sōlum
aedificium, multīs columnīs ōrnātum, manet. tēctum aurō nitidum est.

    lacrimant duo seniōrēs. ubĭ est casa? mox autem cōnsilium deōrum
intellegunt. casa parva nunc templum splendidum est et ipsī custōdēs templī erunt.

Vocabulary

age!	= come!
ānser, ānseris, m.	= goose
custōdiō, -īre	= I guard
līberālitās, -ātis, f.	= generosity
relinquō, -ere, relīquī, relictum	= I leave
respiciō, -ere, respexī, respectum	= I look back
uxor, uxōris, f.	= wife

Detective work

English derivations: perturbed, astute, custodian, summit, region, submerged, edifice.

uxōrī and *marītō*	Look carefully at the endings and remember that they are talking to each other (lines 1 and 2).
vīcīnōs	They live in the vicinity; what do we call them?
aedificium	The noun from *aedificō*. We get the word edifice.
ipsī	Plural of *ipse*.
custōdēs	The noun from *custōdiō*.

Questions

1. What did Philemon say to his wife in line 1?
2. How is his wife described in line 1?
3. What sort of meal did she determine to prepare for the gods (line 2)?
4. Which animal did she decide to kill and what was this animal doing at the time?
5. Why did she not kill the animal in the end (line 4)?
6. Explain why Philemon and Baucis escaped the punishment handed out to their neighbours (lines 4–7).
7. What did the gods order them to do in lines 6–7?
8. What sort of landscape did Philemon and Baucis see when they reached the top of the mountain (line 9)?
9. Describe the building they saw (line 10).
10. What had happened to Philemon's and Baucis's cottage and what happened to the two old people at the end of the story?

Roman food

Now for a spot of food. There's plenty of evidence down below for you to consult and when it comes to translating items of food, just have an inspired guess (yes, *sardae* <u>are</u> sardines and *ostreae* <u>are</u> oysters).

quid edēbant Rōmānī?

dīvitēs famulōs (servōs domesticōs) cibum in culīnā parāre et ad trīclīnium ferre iubēbant. mēnsam sūmptuōsam habēbant – sardās, ostreās, bōlētōs (fungī exquīsītī erant) piscēs vāriōs, carnem multōrum animālium et avium. vīnum aut mulsum (vīnum melle mixtum) bibēbant. amīcōs et comitēs saepe ad cēnam vocābant.

pauperēs nōn carnem sed pānem, lentēs, olīvās, bulbōs, plērumque edēbant. vīnum aquā mixtum bibēbant. diēbus autem fēstīs Rōmānī animālia dīs sacrificābant. pauperēs igitur carnem animālis per tōtum diem edēbant et ventrem complēbant.

et dīvitēs et pauperēs condīmentum, garum nōmine, faciēbant. quōmodo garum fēcērunt? reliquiās piscium in ollā cum sale posuērunt. ibī reliquiae diū manēbant (heu! nāsum teneō! odor nōn placet). tandem – garum est.

Detective work

English derivations –
carnivorous; aviary; exquisite, pauper, nasal, *pain* (French); lentils; condiment.

melle If a voice is mellifluous it is sweet as… Now you know what *mel, mellis*, n. means.

diēbus autem fēstīs = on feast days. *Diēbus* is 5th declension!

Vocabulary

bōlētus, -ī, m.	= a type of mushroom	*plērumque*	= generally
bulbus, -ī, m.	= onion	*pōnō, -ere, posuī, positum*	= I place
comes, -itis, c.	= comrade	*reliquiae, -ārum*, f. pl.	= remains
dīves, dīvitis, c.	= a rich person		
ferō, ferre, tulī, lātum	= I bring	*sal, salis*, m.	= salt
olla, -ae, f.	= jar	*venter, ventris*, m.	= stomach
piscis, piscis, m.	= fish		

48

More Roman food

pauperēs Rōmānī in trīclīniō cīvium dīvitum saepe cēnābant, et semper ventrēs complēbant. ubǐ edere nōn iam poterant, cibum reliquum saepe in mappā magnā pōnēbant. sīc nōn sōlum ūnam cēnam sed duās habēbant!

poēta Mārtiālis nōmine, quī nōn dīves erat, Caeciliānum castīgāvit quod cibum ā mēnsā in mappam trānstulit:

"ūllus sī pudor est, repōne cēnam:
crās tē, Caeciliāne, nōn vocāvī."

poēta Tibullus paene nūllam pecūniam habēbat. puellam pulchram, Dēliam nōmine, amābat et carmen longum scrīpsit:

"cum Dēliā" inquit "mox habitābō. in culīnā labōrāre Dēliae placēbit. ego per tōtum diem legam et scrībam. amīcōs ad convīvia vocābō. Dēlia cibum parābit et ad mēnsam portābit."

ēheu! Dēlia virum dīvitem, nōn Tibullum, amābat. lacrimābat poēta et quod miser erat vīnum bibēbat. sīc scrīpsit:

"saepe ego temptāvī cūrās dēpellere vīnō."

Vocabulary

carmen, carminis, n.	= poem, song
cūra, -ae, f.	= care, worry
mappa, -ae, f.	= napkin
pudor, -ōris, m.	= sense of shame
scrībō, -ere, scrīpsī, scrīptum	= I write
sī	= if

Detective work

trānstulit	Look at the previous vocabulary and you will find that this is a compound of one of the yukkiest perfect stems in the language. Once you have worked out which verb it comes from, the meaning becomes clear.
ūllus sī pudor est...	These lines are genuine Latin verse, so you may need to think extra hard to work them out correctly. The word *repōne* is an order (put back!); the *cēnam* (in the first line) is what Caecilianus has just hidden in his *mappa*; and *nōn vocāvī* means *ad cēnam nōn vocāvī*.
saepe ego	When translating the *Tibullus* line, put at- in front of *temptāvī* to get the English word.
dēpellere	Another way of saying *expellere*.

CHAPTER 9
Imperatives; sentence construction

Cavē!

Before we launch into the next passage, beware! We are going to throw in some new verb forms called imperatives which, as you might be able to work out, are used for giving orders. They are very easy to spot, being formed (for most verbs) from the present stem of the verb (with -*te* on the end if you're speaking to more than one person). Thus, *amā, amāte, monē, monēte, rege, regite, audī, audīte*. So, "*cavē*, my friend!", or should I say "*cavēte*, my friends!".

Daedalus and Icarus

Daedalus erat artifex Athēniēnsis quī opera pulchra et splendida cōnstruēbat. cum fīliō Īcarō ad īnsulam Crētam nāvigāre cōnstituit ubī labyrinthum (hīc Mīnōs rēx Mīnōtaurum cēlābat) magnā arte aedificāvit. nēmō (nisi tandem Thēseus auxiliō Ariadnae) Mīnōtaurum invenīre tūtusque fugere poterat. Daedalus ipse exitum vix inveniēbat. quod autem rēx eum ā Crētā discēdere prohibēbat, fīliō Īcarō "trāns terrās effugere" inquit "nōn possumus, quod Crēta est īnsula, neque trāns mare effugere possumus, quod rēx nōs prohibet. per caelum igitur iter novum faciēmus."

Īcarī auxiliō pinnās et magnās et parvās collēgit. cērā līnōque pinnās ligāvit et mox ālās et pulchrās et validās habēbat.

fīlium iterum iterumque monēbat. "iter" inquit "arduum erit. sōl calidus est, Īcare. sī per caelum altum iter faciēs, sōlis radiī ālās tuās dēlēbunt. medium cursum semper tenē! inter terrās sōlemque semper volā! post mē et prope mē manē! gladium Ōrīōnis vītābimus et…"

(ō pater, tacē, tē implōrō! semper mē monēs. neque cōnsilia neque iussa audīre sed super nūbēs volāre cupiō.)

Vocabulary

āla, -ae, f.	= wing	*ligo, -āre,*	= I tie, bind
artifex, artificis, m.	= craftsman	*-āvī, -ātum*	
calidus, -a, -um	= hot	*līnum, -ī*, n.	= thread
cēra, -ae, f.	= wax	*nisi*	= unless, except
cōnstituō, -ere,	= I decide	*nūbes, -is*, f.	= cloud
cōnstituī, cōnstitūtum		*pinna, -ae*, f.	= feather
inveniō, -īre,	= I find	*que* (at end of word)	= and
invēnī, inventum		*radius, -ī*, m.	= ray
iter, itineris, n.	= journey	*tūtus, -a, -um*	= safe

Detective work

English derivations – prohibit; arduous; construct, collect, medium.

fīliō Īcarō	N.B. It isn't *fīlius Īcarus. cavē!*
gladium Ōrīōnis	Orion (famous for his belt) was a giant hunter before being transformed into a constellation.
iussa	The noun from *iubeō*.

Icarus takes a dive

montem ascendunt novāsque ālās pater umerīs fīlī accommodat. dum labōrat 1
genae lacrimīs ūmidae sunt. tandem ālae parātae sunt et in caelum ascendunt
et pater et fīlius. prīmō tūtī per caelum prōcēdunt. Daedalus "ecce!" inquit
"sinistrā sunt īnsulae Samos Dēlosque, dextrā Sporadēs. mox ad Graeciam
adveniēmus." incolae īnsulārum, agricolae piscātōrēsque, ubī duās figūrās 5
novās in caelō vident, Daedalī mīrum opus nōn intellegunt. "dī sunt," inquiunt.

"dī nostrī opera mīra facere possunt."
saepe respicit Daedalus fīliumque tūtum esse videt. subitō
autem Īcarus "iter longum est" inquit. "mē taedet." tandem,
quod taedium relevāre cupit, patris iussa neglegit et ad 10
sōlem ascendit.
mox cēra liquida est puerque territus in undās cadit.
Daedalus "Īcare," inquit, "Īcare, ubī es? ubī es? num
mea verba neglēxistī?"
mare spectat. nihil nisi pinnās videt. 15

Vocabulary

accommodō, -āre	=	I fit
gena, -ae, f.	=	cheek
piscātor, -ōris, m.	=	fisherman
ūmidus, -a, -um	=	wet

Detective work

English derivations – sporadic (from the Greek islands, Sporades); tedium; neglect.

taedet An example of an impersonal verb; it wearies, i.e. it is a bore!

Questions on Icarus takes a dive

1. What did the father do with the new wings in line 1?
2. How do we know that Daedalus was feeling rather emotional at this time in lines 1–2?
3. What did Daedalus point out to his son on the left in line 4?
4. What did he point out on the right in line 4?
5. What did the farmers and fishermen think when they saw the figures of Daedalus and Icarus passing across the sky in lines 5–7?
6. Why did Icarus decide to fly upwards towards the sun in lines 9–11?
7. Why was this a disastrous move on his part in lines 12–13?
8. Describe the sight Daedalus saw when he looked at the sea in the last line.

Eureka!

Did somebody in very early times really invent a hang-glider, which was abandoned because of a terrible accident on its maiden flight? We don't know. However there were real-life inventors that we do know about. One of the most famous is Archimedes, who is supposed to have discovered specific gravity while in his bath, causing him to emit the triumphant shriek "**Eureka!**" (Greek for "I have discovered").

Archimēdēs cīvis Syrācūsānus erat. atavōs autem, quod Syrācūsās multaque alia Siciliae oppida Graecī condidērunt, Graecōs nōn Rōmānōs habēbat. artēs mathēmaticās per tōtam vītam amābat multōsque librōs dē sphaerā cylindrōque scrīpsit.

ōlim dum sē lavat, dē pondere et aquae et corporis suī cōgitāvit. subitō magnā vōce exclāmāvit "εὕρηκα!" et per viās urbis cucurrit.

multās quoque et mīrās māchinās fēcit. ingeniō enim suō aquam ē flūminibus ad collēs dūxit. agricolae igitur quī clīvōs colēbant (quod agrōs irrigāre nunc poterant) grātiam hominī ērudītō et ingeniōsō habēbant.

Vocabulary

atavus, -ī, m.	= ancestor
clīvus, -ī, m.	= slope, hillside
collis, collis, m.	= hill
condō, -ere,	= I found, establish
condidī, conditum	
flūmen, flūminis, n.	= river
pondus,	= weight
ponderis, n.	
suus, -a, -um	= his, her, its, their

εὕρηκα!

Detective work

Derivations: Art, mathematics, sphere, cylinder, cogitate, machine, ingenuity and genius, irrigate, erudite. We even get lavatory from *lavō*!

Syrācūsānus/Syrācūsās	Syracuse is a city in Sicily.
atavōs autem…habēbat	This sentence looks hard, but is easy provided that you pick out the subjects and objects carefully.
sē lavat	Reflexives in Latin are no problem if you think of how French works; e.g. *il se lave*.
corporis suī	*Suus* in Latin means his, her, its or their, referring back to the subject of the sentence.
εὕρηκα!	Now you know some Greek!
colēbant	*agricolae* are so called because *agrōs colunt*.

Archimedes' unfortunate death

etiam in bellō Archimēdēs ingenium artemque praebēbat. dum enim Rōmānī 1
Syrācūsās obsident māchinās et ballistās fēcit quae saxa magnī ponderis
trāns moenia urbis in nāvēs Rōmānās iniciēbant. sīc cīvēs urbem diū
dēfendere poterant.

ubĭ Rōmānī urbem tandem cēpērunt, Mārcellus, imperātor Rōmānus, 5
Archimēdis ingeniō attonitus, quod māchinās et ballistās novās cognōscere
volēbat, mīlitem ad eum mīsit et ad castra Rōmāna invītāvit. ille autem figūrās
mathēmaticās in pulvere dēscrībēbat et propter amōrem scientiae mīlitem
neque accipere neque audīre volēbat. mīles autem, īrātus quod philosophus
iussa imperātōris iterum iterumque neglegēbat, eum gladiō tandem necāvit. 10
nōn sōlum cīvēs Syrācūsānī sed etiam Mārcellus multīque Rōmānī,
quamquam Archimēdēs hostis erat, mortem tamen miseram maerēbant.

Vocabulary

amor, amōris, m.   = love
cognōscō, -ere   = I learn about
imperātor, -ōris, m. = general
moenia, -um, n. pl. = city walls
obsideō, -ēre,   = I besiege
  obsēdī, obsessum
pulvis, pulveris, m. = dust
saxum, -ī, n.   = rock

Detective work

English derivations: ballistic, navy,
science, philosopher, military, describe.

iniciēbant = in + iaciēbant

ille   Think of the French word *il*.

quae The feminine form of *quī*.

Questions on Archimedes' unfortunate death

1. How did Archimedes demonstrate his usefulness in wartime?
2. Who was the Roman general and what was his opinion of Archimedes?
3. Why was a Roman soldier sent to Archimedes and what was the message he took with him?
4. Why did Archimedes not respond promptly to the arrival of the soldier?
5. How did the soldier react to the delay?
6. How was news of the death of Archimedes received by the citizens of Syracuse?
7. How was news of the death of Archimedes received by the Romans?

Roman legacies

Although the Greeks produced more philosophers, dramatists and artists than the Romans, we owe a great debt to the Romans for their engineering and practical skills, which they used not just in Rome but throughout the empire.

Legacy 1

Here is a particularly useful legacy from the Romans. Fill in the blanks to find out what it is:

> *Rōmānī multās —— per tōtum imperium mūnīvērunt. longae rēctaeque erant. legiōnēs Rōmānae per eās magna itinera faciēbant. omnēs ——— Rōmam ferēbant, praesertim —— Appia et —— Flāminia et ——— Aurēlia.*

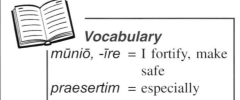

Detective work

English derivations: direct, legions.

magna itinera: strictly speaking, *magnum iter* is the Latin for a forced march.

Rōmam ferēbant: remember, we have a saying: "All —— lead to Rome."

Vocabulary

mūniō, -īre = I fortify, make safe

praesertim = especially

Legacy 2

And here is another.

Graecī, quamquam templa pulchra cōnstrūxērunt, tēctum tamen columnīs altīs rēctīsque, nōn arcibus curvīs sustinēbant. Rōmānī autem, quod arcūs excolere cōnstituērunt, aedificia magna et splendida tēctō concavō cōnstruere poterant. prīncipēs Rōmānī multōs arcūs triumphālēs post victōriam aedificāvērunt quōrum trēs, Arcūs Titī et Cōnstantīnī et Septimī Sevērī etiam nunc paene integrī sunt.

Detective work

Useful derivations: curved, sustain, concave, triumphal, Arc de Triomphe.

cōnstrūxērunt The supine of this verb is *cōnstrūctum*, so you can work out what it means.

arcūs The word *arcus* is a 4th declension noun. Don't panic, it's not difficult; you'll cope! 4th declension nouns go *-ūs* in the nominative, vocative and accusative plural.

prīncipēs This title was given to the Roman Emperors.

quōrum The ending (*-ōrum*) is clearly genitive plural and its from your old friend *quī* = who or which.

Vocabulary

altus, -a, -um	= high
excolō, -ere, excoluī, excultum	= I improve, make perfect
integer, integra, integrum	= whole, intact

CHAPTER 10
The future-perfect and pluperfect tenses

Action-packed lives

Once you have learned the pluperfect and future perfect tenses you have covered the whole range of time: past, present and future. In the passages below the verbs are in different tenses and cover the person's whole career. The present tense (in bold type) indicates mid-career. Can you say who these colourful characters are? Some are mythological and some historical (you may need to look up some details in a dictionary of mythology).

1) *saepe opera difficilia suscipiēbat. multa capita Hydrae interfēcit. iam serpentēs, quamquam īnfāns erat, strangulāverat.* **nunc stabula Augēae pūrgat.** *mox ad regiōnēs īnfernās dēscendet Cerberumque capiet. bovēs Gēryonis iam cēperit.*

Detective work

bovēs	Our word bovine (as in B.S.E.) comes from this.
suscipiō	A compound of *sub* and *capiō*. Translate both and put them together and you have the English verb.
interfēcit	The trick is less helpful here. Although coming from *inter* and *faciō*, translate this verb as if it were *necō* and you should be okay.
regiōnēs īnfernās	
	Our phrase infernal regions isn't bad here; *īnfernus* means lower.

2) *rēx erat duxque Graecōrum. trāns mare secundīs ventīs nāvigāvit. iam fīliam deae sacrificāverat.* **nunc cum Troiānīs pugnat.** *mox uxor eum interficiet. iam Cassandra rēgis mortem futūram praedīxerit.*

Vocabulary

mors, mortis, f.	= death
secundus, -a, -um	= following, favourable
uxor, -ōris, f.	= wife

3) *patrem suum, dum iter Thēbās facit, interfēcit. iam ōrāculum eum Corinthō discēdere iusserat.* **nunc in urbe habitat.** *mox mātrem suam in mātrimōnium dūcet et rēx Thēbanōrum erit. iam aenigma solverit.*

Detective work

You've met *meus* and *tuus*. *Suus* is used as the 3rd person adjective.

Thēbās and *Corinthō* – it was customary not to use prepositions with names of towns and small islands, so how do you know which way they were going? By looking at the ending, of course, and deciding on the case:

ACCUSATIVE – TOWARDS   ABLATIVE – FROM

aenigma An enigma is a riddle.

4) *Troiānus erat quī cum Graecīs pugnābat. ubǐ Graecī urbem Troiam cēpērunt, patrem fīliumque parvum ē perīculō servāvit. māter Venus iam eum monuerat.* **nunc trāns maria ad multās terrās nāvigat.** *mox ad Ītaliam adveniet. iam in urbe Carthāgine mānserit rēgīnamque amāverit.*

5) *Saguntum obsidēbat et tandem cēpit. pater enim puerum iam ad Hispāniam dūxerat.* **nunc trāns montēs cum elephantīs prōcēdit.** *mox prope urbem Rōmam cum mīlitibus pugnābit. iam multās victōriās pepererit.*

Vocabulary

Saguntum, -ī, n.	A city in Spain
victōriam pariō, -ere, =	I win a victory
peperī, partum	

6) *atavus erat prīmus cōnsul. cōnsilium cum collēgīs cēperat Caesaremque Īdibus Mārtiīs interfēcit.* **nunc exsul in Macedoniā est.** *mox sē gladiō interficiet. iam Mārcus Antōnius et Octāviānus eum in proeliō vīcerint.*

Detective work

If you have **atavistic** tendencies, you take after your ancestors.

cōnsilium cēperat	He didn't capture a plan, he adopted one.
Īdibus Mārtiīs	A very famous date in Roman history.
vīcerint	Remember Caesar's famous words: *vēnī, vīdī, vīcī.*

Meet Fabius

Were there any famous detectives in ancient Rome? We don't know of any, though there were real spies and informers under the less pleasant Emperors. So let's invent one. His name is FABIUS and he can solve ANYTHING. You can match him, can't you? You naturally interpret this as a *NŌNNE* question and answer YES – though you may have to look some things up in a reference book.

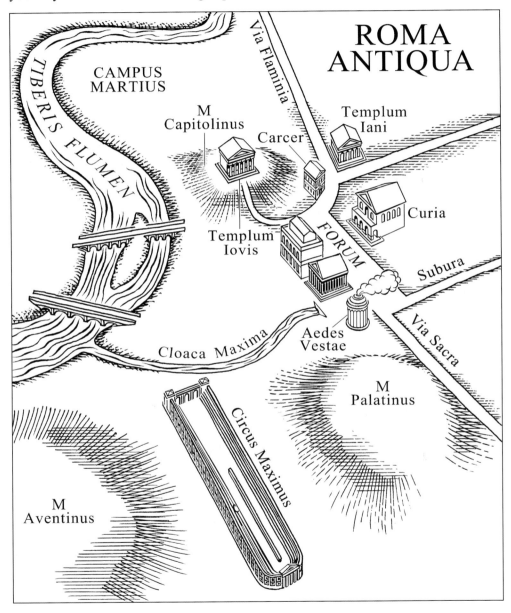

Cūria: The Seanate House; *Aedes Vestae*: The Temple of Vesta;
Cloāca Maxima: The main drain in Rome; *Carcer*: The prison;
Templum Iovis: The Temple of Jupiter; *Templum Iānī*: The Temple of Janus.

The grand chase through Rome

On the small plan of ancient Rome you will see marked some of the city's most important areas: the Campus Martius, in early times the exercise ground of Roman armies; the temple of Jupiter Optimus Maximus on the Capitoline Hill; the temple of Janus, the two-headed god, where the doors were open in time of war and closed in time of peace; the senate house and forum; the temple of Vesta, where the sacred fire, on which Rome's safety depended, was kept continually alight by the Vestal Virgins. The Sacred Way led up to this important area. A short distance away, towards the Aventine Hill, was the Circus Maximus, where chariot races and shows were held.

ōlim Fabius, ubĭ in Campō Mārtiō cum amīcīs lūdēbat, subitō hominem rūfum   1
cōnspexit quī trāns Campum currēbat. mox turbam cīvium vīdit quī flūmen
Tiberim petēbant et, dum currunt, "Fabī," inquiunt, " vix spīrāre possumus –
hominemne rūfum cōnspexistī? nuper enim – dum in Monte Capitōlīnō
ambulāmus – hominem vīdimus – quī statuam Rōmulī Remīque dēlēbat.   5
partem lupae iam frēgerat. per septem collēs cucurrimus – neque eum
cēpimus. ēheu! fortasse iam effūgerit. nōs adiuvā, Fabī, tē implōrāmus."

    Fabius "hominem rūfum" inquit "nūper cōnspexī. ille nec flūmen Tiberim
nec viam Flāminiam sed Montem Capitōlīnum petēbat. ē Campō iam
discesserit. ad Capitōlium! celeriter!"   10

    Fabius comitēsque eō magnā celeritāte festīnant et mox Fabius "rubrōs"
inquit "capillōs videō. Fortūna nōbīs favet."

    ūnus ē Fabiī comitibus "sī dea Fortūna" inquit "nōbīs fāverit, homo fortasse
cadet. sī ceciderit tībiamque frēgerit, eum capiēmus."

    Fabius "eum" inquit "aut fortūnā aut ingeniō nostrō capiēmus. ecce! dē   15
Capitōliō dēscendit."

Vocabulary

cōnspiciō, -ere,	= I catch sight of	*petō, -ere,*	= I seek, head for
-spexī, -spectum		*-īvī, -ītum*	
eō	= there, to that place	*ruber, rubra,*	= red, ruddy
lupa, -ae, f.	= she-wolf	*rubrum*	
nūper	= recently	*rūfus, -a, -um*	= red-headed

17   *omnēs celeriter currunt et hominem petunt. ille autem carcerem, templum Iānī, cūriam sinistrā relinquit et per forum ad Viam Sacram currit. subitō, ubĭ paene in manibus Fabiī comitumque est, prope aedem Vestae in viam dextram*
20 *festīnat et…*
      ubĭ est?
      neque hominem neque hominis vestīgia vident. comitēs Fabiō "sine dubiō" inquiunt "effūgit. ubĭ est?"
      Fabius autem, quī vir acūtō ingeniō erat, "bene sciō" inquit. "neque in viīs
25 *neque in aedificiīs homŏ est. Circum Maximum non petet quod ibĭ sē cēlāre nōn poterit. ālās nōn habet neque in caelō est. ubĭ igitur est? quid rēgēs nostrī hīc cōnstrūxērunt? quid necessārium est sānitātī cīvium? odor nōn placēbit sed dēscendēmus. dēscendere est facile sed, ut dīcit poēta Vergilius, "revocāre gradum superāsque ēvādere ad aurās, hoc opus, hic labor est."*

Vocabulary

aedis, -is, f.	=	small temple
sciō, -īre	=	I know
sine (+ abl.)	=	without

Detective work

English derivations – civilian, dubious, ingenuity, incarcerated, vestige, acute, sanitation.

When you see *Fabiō* (line 22) before inverted commas, investigate his ending and THINK HARD.

Fabius liked to show off a bit and in the last sentence he is quoting from Vergil's Aeneid. The priestess of the oracle told Aeneas, who wanted to go down to the Underworld to visit his father, that going down was easy but "to retrace one's step and to escape to the air above, this is the task, this is the hard work."

Questions

1. Describe carefully the route taken by the man escaping from Fabius and the crowd (lines 4–21).

2. Where did the man disappear from sight in lines 19–20?

3. Why did Fabius consider that the man was not in the Circus Maximus in lines 25–26?

4. Where did Fabius think the man had gone (lines 24–29)? Look carefully at the map.

5. Why did he say *odor nōn placēbit* in lines 27–28?

In the baths

If you think a Leisure Centre is a new idea, you're wrong. The Romans had already thought of it and built BALNEAE or THERMAE all over the Empire. Just before the birth of Christ there were 170 public baths in Rome. Even in a remote part of the Empire like Britain there were baths. What do we call the Roman spa of Aquae Sulis? Yes – BATH. If there were no hot springs to hand, they used the HYPOCAUST system for underfloor heating.

Wealthier Romans often had similar facilities in their own homes and would probably enjoy showing off their new bathroom, just as some of us do today. But everyone could go to the public baths as the entrance fee was so small. Some of these establishments would be quite simple but later they became huge and ornate with all kinds of leisure activity. The Baths of Caracalla and Diocletian offered massage rooms, gyms, exercise rooms, rest rooms, reading rooms where an author could recite his latest work, promenades, gardens, shops, and of course snack bars, complete with sausages. No wonder the Romans used the Baths as a social club.

Bathers would get changed in the APODYTERIUM (changing room). They would then exercise in the PALAESTRA before moving through into the baths themselves. The bathing area would have a TEPIDARIUM (warm room), a CALDARIUM (hot room) where you had a 'good sweat' and a FRIGIDARIUM (cold room) where you took a refreshing plunge. Fabius loved the Baths!

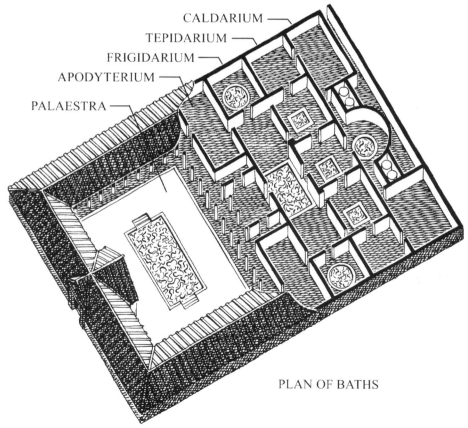

CALDARIUM
TEPIDARIUM
FRIGIDARIUM
APODYTERIUM
PALAESTRA

PLAN OF BATHS

Fabius needs a plan…

herī Fabius ad thermās ambulāre cōnstituit. prīdiē quoque ad thermās
ambulāverat. paene cotīdiē eō ambulābat ibīque cum amīcīs corpus recreābat.

dum vestīmenta servī auxiliō exuit, Quīntum amīcum cōnspexit quī "salvē"
inquit "mī Fabī. hodiē amīcus carmen novum in thermīs recitābit. amīcī
carmina semper pulchra sunt cīvēsque semper dēlectant. tē magnō gaudiō
invītō."

Fabius nihil dīxit. carmina amīcī Quīntī semper longa erant neque Fabiō
placēbant. quamquam domum statim festīnāre cupīvit, Quīntum tamen
offendere nōlēbat. grātiās igitur amīcō ēgit.

dum servī corpus Fabiī oleō ungēbant manibusque pulsābant ille
dēlīberābat: quōmodo taedium vītābō? ō mē miserum! sed causa bona
(fortasse falsa – dī, misericordiam vestram implōrō) mox in mentem veniet.

Fabius has a plan!

in tepidāriō diū manēbat, sed frūstrā. quod multī clāmōrēs circumsonābant, 1
nūllum cōnsilium cēpit. in caldāriō quoque diū manēbat sed calor vaporque
mentem superāvērunt. tandem in piscīnam frīgidam saluit. ecce! mēns
recreāta est et statim cōnsilium cēpit.

mox Quīntī amīcus carmen longum recitābat. multī iam obdormīverant 5
sed Fabius multā urbānitāte audiēbat. subitō sternuit. atishoo. iterum sternuit.
atishoo. deinde ter sternuit; ē sellā surgit.

"quam īnfēlīx – atishoo – mī Quīnte, – atishoo – sum. carmen pulchrum –
atishoo – nunc audīre nōn possum. sed amīcus tuus – atishoo – est fēlīx –
atishoo. sīc enim sternuere est bonum ōmen – atishoo. **sternuō** 10
approbātiōnem, ut dīcit Catullus poēta. ATISHOO."

celeriter exit et ad palaestram festīnat. num sternuit Fabius in palaestrā?
quid tū putās?

Questions on Fabius has a plan

1. Why was Fabius unable to think of a good idea while he was in the *tepidārium*? (Lines 1–2)

2. Why was he unable to think of a good idea in the *caldārium*? (Lines 2–3)

3. Where was it that Fabius was eventually able to think clearly and why was this? (Lines 3–4)

4. In line 5, what was the reaction of the audience to the recital of Quintus' friend?

5. What was Fabius' plan for escaping the ordeal of listening to the poet? (Lines 4–11)

6. Where did Fabius go to get away from the poetry recital? (Line 12)

Vocabulary

calor, calōris, m.	= heat	*palaestra, -ae,* f.	= exercise ground
misericordia, -ae, f.	= pity, mercy	*prīdiē*	= the day before
nihil	= nothing	*sella, -ae,* f.	= chair
obdormīscō, -ere, obdormīvī	= I go to sleep	*sternuō, -ere, -uī*	= I sneeze
		vapor, -ōris, m.	= steam
oleum, -ī, n.	= oil		

Detective work

English derivations – tedium; deliberate (as a verb); prohibit; urbanity; approbation.

exuit	If *indūtus* means dressed, from *induō*, what will *exuō* mean?
mī	Remember, this is the vocative of *meus*.
nōlēbat	The verb *volō* means I wish. *nōlō* is the exact opposite (*nōn volō*).
ungēbant and *pulsābant*	Fabius is having the 'health treatment' so think what the slaves would be doing.
saluit	What will *in* mean with the accusative after it? Now you know what *saliō* must mean.
sternuō approbātiōnem	I sneeze approval. The phrase comes from a poem by Catullus where two young lovers are declaring eternal devotion to each other. Cupid keeps "sneezing approval".
exit	From *exeō* = I go out.

Another problem in the Baths: 1

palaestra plēna erat cīvibus quī omnēs magnā vōce clāmābant. inter clāmōrēs tumultumque Fabius Valerium amīcum cōnspexit quī "nōnne carmen novum" inquit "mī Fabī, audīre dēbēs? num aeger es?"

Fabius "nōn aeger sum" inquit "sed paene īnsānus sum. carmina misera vetāre dēbēmus. sīc enim īnsāniam vītābimus. sed cūr in palaestrā tantus tumultus tantaque īnsānia est?"

respondit amīcus: "fūrēs in balneās intrāvērunt. octŏ pōcula aurea multamque pecūniam abstulērunt. hīc in balneīs latent neque eōs invenīre possumus. auxilium ā tē, Fabī, petimus."

prīmum in caldārium Fabius cum amīcō intrat ubĭ dormiunt quattuor senātōrēs nōtī. "saepe stultī" inquit "nōn autem fūrēs sunt." deinde in tepidārium prōcēdit ubĭ servī corpora cīvium oleō ungunt manibusque pulsant. omnēs cīvēs et Fabiō et amīcō nōtī sunt. tandem ad piscīnam prōcēdit et amīcō "trēs videō" inquit "quī in piscīnā natant. quī sunt?" amīcus "eōs iam interrogāvimus" inquit. "cīvis Rōmānus cum duōbus fīliīs est. fīliōs natāre dēlectat. alter ūndecim, alter tredecim annōs habet."

Another problem in the Baths: 2

trēs togās quae prope piscīnam iacēbant Fabius subitō cōnspexit. tōtae albae erant. "fortasse" inquit " fūrēs in piscīnā natant. fortasse pōcula et pecūnia cum fūribus latent. vērum enim hominēs nōn dīxērunt. cūr togae hīc iacent? cūr togās in apodytēriō nōn exuērunt? togae tōtae albae sunt. duo igitur fīliī nōn puerī parvī sunt…"

Valerius "vērum dīcis" inquit. "tantum ingenium, mī Fabī, mentemque tam acūtam habēs."

Fabius "mentem nōn sōlum acūtam sed praesertim sānam nunc cupiō. mēns sāna in corpore sānō, ut dīcit poēta Iuvenālis, hominibus bonum est."

Vocabulary

apodytērium, -ī, n.	= changing room.	lateō, -ēre, -uī	= I lie hidden
deinde	= then	pecūnia, -ae, f.	= money
fūr, fūris, m.	= thief	tantus, -a, -um	= so much, so great

Detective work

Derivations: tumult, respond, proceed, interrogate.

abstulērunt	the *-tulērunt* should tell you this verb is a form of our old friend *ferō*. Look up *auferō* in the back to find your answer.
mēns sāna in corpore sānō	This is a famous phrase from one of the poet Juvenal's satires. It has become a well known saying or "tag".
bonum	When *bonus* is used alone (i.e. without a noun) in the masculine, it means a good man; when it is used in the feminine it means a good woman. What do you think it means when used in the neuter?

Questions

Make sure you have read and understood the whole passage: *Another problem in the Baths*. Then answer the following questions on part 2 of the story.

1. What did Fabius see near the pool?
2. What did Fabius say about the three men in the pool?
3. Why was Fabius surprised that the togas were lying beside the pool?
4. What was it about the togas themselves which attracted Fabius' attention?
5. And now for some real detective work; how did Fabius know that the three swimmers were all adults? You may have to refer back to our section on Roman clothes to answer this.

Vocabulary

ā, ab (+ abl.) = by, from
abeō, -īre, abiī, abitum = I go away
absum, abesse, āfuī (goes like *sum*) = I am absent
accidit, -ere, accidit = it happens
accipiō, -ere, accēpī, acceptum = I receive
accommodō, -āre, -āvī, -ātum = I fit
accūsō, -āre, -āvī, -ātum = I accuse
acūtus, -a, -um = sharp
ad (+ acc.) = to, towards
adiuvō, -āre, adiūvī, adiūtum = I help
adōrō, -āre, -āvī, -ātum = I adore
adsum, adesse, adfuī (goes like *sum*) = I am present
adulēscēns, adulēscentis, c. = young person, young man
adultus, -a, -um = adult, grown up
adveniō, -īre, advēnī, adventum = I arrive
aedificium, -iī, n. = building
aedificō, -āre, -āvī, -ātum = I build
aedis, aedis, f. = house, small temple
aeger, aegra, aegrum = sick
aegrē (adverb) = with difficulty
Aenēās, -ae, m. (voc. *Aenēā*, acc. *Aenēān*) = Aeneas
aenigma, aenigmatis, n. = riddle
aestās, aestātis, f. = summer
aestuārium, -iī, n. = estuary
aeternus, -a, -um = eternal
age! = come!
ager, agrī, m. = field
agō, agere, ēgī, āctum = I do, drive
agricola, -ae, m. = farmer
agricultūra, -ae, f. = agriculture
āla, -ae, f. = wing
albus, -a, -um = white
aliī...aliī = some...others
aliter = otherwise
alius, alia, aliud = other

alter, altera, alterum = the other (of two)
alter...alter = the one...the other
altus, -a, -um = deep, high
ambulō, -āre, -āvī, -ātum = I walk
amīca, -ae, f. = girl friend
amīcus, -ī, m. = friend
amō, amāre, amāvī, amātum = I love, like
amor, amōris, m. = love
āmoveō, -ēre, āmōvī, āmōtum = I withdraw, steal
animal, animālis, n. = animal
annus, -ī, m. = year
ānser, ānseris, m. = goose
ante (+ acc.) = before (preposition)
anteā = beforehand, previously
antīquus, -a, -um = old, antique, ancient
aperiō, -īre, -uī, apertum = I open
apertus, -a, -um = open
appāreō, -ēre, -uī, -itum = I appear
approbātiō, -ōnis, f. = approval
appropinquō, -āre, -āvī, -ātum (+ dat. or *ad* + acc.) = I approach
aptus, -a, -um = suitable
apud (+ acc.) = at the house of, among, at, near
aqua, -ae, f. = water
aquila, -ae, f. = eagle
āra, -ae, f. = altar
arānea, -ae, f. = spider
arbor, -ŏris, f. = tree
arcus, -ūs, m. = arch
arduus, -a, -um = steep, difficult
argentum, -ī, n. = silver
arma, -ōrum, n. pl. = weapons
armātus, -a, -um = armed
arō, -āre, -āvī, -ātum = I plough
arrogantia, -ae, f. = arrogance
ars, artis, f. = skill, art
artifex, artificis, m. = craftsman

ascendō, -ere, ascendī, ascēnsum = I climb

asinus, -ī, m. = ass

āstūtus, -a, -um = clever

atavus, -ī, m. = ancestor

Athēnae, -ārum, f. pl. = Athens

Athēniēnsis, -e = Athenian

atque = and

ātrium, ātriī, n. = hall

attonitus, -a, -um = amazed

audāx, audācis = bold

audācter (adverb) = boldly

audiō, -īre, -īvī, -ītum = I hear, listen to

auferō, auferre, abstulī, ablātum = I carry away, steal

augeō, -ēre, auxī, auctum = I increase

augustus, -a, -um = venerable, majestic

aura, -ae, f. = breeze, air

aureus, -a, -um = golden

auris, auris, f. = ear

aurum, -ī, n. = gold

aut = or

aut...aut = either...or

autem = however, moreover (not written 1st word in clause)

auxilium, -iī, n. = help

avis, avis, f. = bird

avunculus, -ī, m. = uncle

avus, -ī, m. = grandfather

ballista, -ae, f. = ballista, catapult

balneae, -ārum, f. pl. = baths

barba, -ae, f. = beard

bellum, -ī, n. = war

bene = well

benignus, -a, -um = kind

bibliothēca, -ae, f. = library

bibō, -ere, bibī = I drink

bis (adverb) = twice

bōlētus, -ī, m. = mushroom

bona, -ōrum, n. pl = goods

bonus, -a, -um = good

bōs, bovis, c. (irreg.) = ox, cow

Britannus, -a, -um = British

bulbus, -ī, m. = onion

cadō, -ere, cecidī, cāsum = I fall

caelicola, -ae, c. = god

caelum, -ī, n. = sky, weather

caeruleus, -a, -um = sky-blue

calamus, -ī, m. = reed

caldārium, -iī, n. = hot room (in the baths)

calidus, -a, -um = hot

callidus, -a, -um = skilful, crafty

calor, calōris, m. = heat

campus, -ī, m. = plain

Camulodūnum, -ī, n. = Colchester

canis, canis, c. = dog

canō, -ere, cecinī, cantum = I sing

cantō, -āre, -āvī, -ātum = I sing

capillus, -ī, m. = hair

capiō, -ere, cēpī, captum = I take, capture

captīvus, -ī, m. = prisoner

captō, -āre, -āvī, -ātum = I chase

caput, capitis, n. = head

carcer, -eris, m. = prison

carmen, carminis, n. = poem, song

carō, carnis, f. = flesh, meat

carpentum, -ī, n. = carriage

cārus, -a, -um = dear

casa, -ae, f. = cottage

castīgō, -āre, -āvī, -ātum = I punish, chastise

castra pōnō = I pitch a camp

castra, -ōrum, n. pl. = camp

causa, -ae, f. = cause, reason

caveō, -ēre, cāvī, cautum (+ acc.) = I am cautious (of)

cecidī: see *cadō*

celer, celeris, celere = swift, quick

celeritās, celeritātis, f. = speed

celeriter = quickly

cēlō, -āre, -āvī, -ātum = I hide (trans.)

cēna, -ae, f. = dinner

cēnō, -āre, -āvī, -ātum = I dine

centum = one hundred

cēpī: see *capiō*

cēra, -ae, f. = wax

certus, -a, -um = certain

cerva, -ae, f. = deer, hind

cēterī, -ae, -a = other, remaining

cibus, -ī, m. = food

cīnctus, -a, -um = surrounded

circiter (adverb) = around

circum (+ acc.) = around

circumsonō, -āre, -uī, -itum = I resound

cīvis, cīvis, c. = citizen

clāmō, -āre, -āvī, -ātum = I shout

clāmor, -ōris, m. = shout

clārus, -a, -um = famous

claudō, claudere, clausī, clausum = I close

clīvus, -ī, m. = slope, hillside

coēgī: see *cōgō*

cōgitō, -āre, -āvī, -ātum = I think, consider

cognōscō, -ere, cognōvī, cognitum = I learn, find out

cōgō, cōgere, coēgī, coāctum = I compel, force

collēga, -ae, m. = colleague

colligō, -ere, collēgī, collēctum = I collect

collis, collis, m. = hill

collocō, -āre, -āvī, -ātum = I place

collum, -ī, n. = neck

colō, colere, coluī, cultum = I cultivate, worship

Colossēum, - ī, n. = amphitheatre in Rome

columna, -ae, f. = column, pillar

comes, comitis, c. = companion

commodus, -a, -um = suitable, commodious

comparō, -āre, -āvī, -ātum = I get ready, prepare (trans.)

compleō, -ēre, complēvī, complētum = I fill

compluvium, -ī, n. = compluvium, a hole in the roof of the atrium to let rainwater in

comportō, -āre, -āvī, -ātum = I carry together, collect

concavus, -a, -um = concave

condīmentum, -ī, n. = spicy sauce, relish

condō, -ere, condidī, conditum = I found (a city)

cōnfirmō, -āre, -āvī, -ātum = I confirm

cōnsilium, -iī, n. = plan

cōnsilium capiō = I adopt a plan

cōnspiciō, -ere, cōnspexī, cōnspectum = I catch sight of

cōnstituō, -ere, cōnstituī, cōnstitūtum = I decide, settle, station

cōnstruō, -ere, cōnstrūxī, cōnstrūctum = I construct, build

cōnsul, cōnsulis, m. = consul

contemnō, -ere, contempsī, contemptum = I despise

contrā (+ acc.) = against

conveniō, -īre, convēnī, conventum = I come together

convertō, -ere, convertī, conversum = I turn around (trans.)

convīvium, -iī, n. = feast

cōpiae, -ārum, f. pl. = forces

coquus, -ī, m. = cook

corōna, -ae, f. = crown, garland

corōnātus, -a, -um = crowned, garlanded

corpus, -ŏris, n. = body

coruscō, -āre, -āvī, -ātum = I gleam

cotīdiē (or *cottīdiē*) = every day

crās = tomorrow

crēdō, -ere, crēdidī, crēditum (+ dat.) = I trust, believe

crēscō, -ere, crēvī, crētum = I grow

Crēta, -ae, f. = Crete

cubiculum, -ī, n. = bedroom

cucurbita, -ae, f. = gourd, cucumber

cucurrī: see *currō*

culīna, -ae, f. = kitchen
culpō, -āre, -āvī, -ātum = I blame
cum (+ abl.) = with, together with
cūnctus, -a, -um = all
cupiō, -ere, -īvī, -ītum = I want, desire
cūr? = why?
cūra, -ae, f. = care
cūria, -ae, f. = senate-house
cūrō, -āre, -āvī, -ātum = I care for
currō, -ere, cucurrī, cursum = I run
currus, -ūs, m. = chariot
cursus, -ūs, m. = course, journey
curvus, -a, -um = curved
custōdiō, -īre, -īvī, -ītum = I guard
custōs, custōdis, c. = guard
cylindrus, -ī, m. = cylinder
damnō, -āre, -āvī, -ātum = I condemn, sentence to punishment
dē (+ abl.) = down from, concerning
dea, -ae, f. = goddess (dat. and abl. pl. = *deābus*)
dēbeō, -ēre, -uī, -itum = I ought, owe
decem = ten
dedī: see *dō*
dēfendō, -ere, dēfendī, dēfēnsum = I defend
dēficiō, -ere, dēfēcī, dēfectum = I fail, run short
deinde = then
dēlectō, -āre, -āvī, -ātum = I delight, please
dēleō, dēlēre, dēlēvī, dēlētum = I destroy
dēlīberō, -āre, -āvī, -ātum = I deliberate, ponder
dēnārius, -iī, m. (gen. pl. regularly *dēnārium*) = denarius (a coin)
dēnique (adverb) = then, at length
dēns, dentis, m. = tooth
dēnsus, -a, -um = thick
dēpellō, -ere, -pulī, -pulsum = I drive out

dēscendō, -ere, dēscendī, dēscēnsum = I go down
dēscrībō, -ere, dēscrīpsī, dēscrīptum = I describe, draw
dēsīderō, -āre, -āvī, -ātum = I long for
dēsiliō, -īre, dēsiluī = I leap down
dēspērō, -āre, -āvī, -ātum = I despair
dētergeō, -ēre, dētersī, dētersum = I wipe clean
dētineō, -ēre, dētinuī, dētentum = I hold back
deus, deī, m. (irreg.) = god
dēvolō, -āre, -āvī, -ātum = I fly down
dēvorō, -āre, -āvī, -ātum = I devour
dexter, dextra, dextrum (or *dexter, dextera, dexterum*) = right (as opposed to left)
dextra, -ae, f. = right hand
dextrā = on the right
dī: part of *deus*
dīcō, dīcere, dīxī, dictum = I say
didicī: see *discō*
diēs, diēī, m. = day (f. if an appointed day)
difficilis, -e = difficult
digitus, -ī, m. = finger
dīligēns, -entis = careful
dīligenter = carefully
dīrus, -a, -um = terrible
discēdō, -ere, discessī, discessum = I depart
discipulus, -ī, m. / *discipula, -ae*, f. = pupil
discō, -ere, didicī = I learn
diū (adverb) = for a long time
diūtius (adverb) = for a longer time
dīves, dīvitis = rich (as noun = a rich man)
dīvidō, -ere, dīvīsī, dīvīsum = I divide
dīvīnō, -āre, -āvī, -ātum = I foresee
dīvīnus, -a, -um = divine

dīvitiae, -ārum, f. pl. = riches, wealth

dīvulgō, -āre, -āvī, -ātum = I divulge, publish

dīvus, -ī, m. (gen. pl.: **dīvum**) = a god

dīxī: see **dīcō**

dō, dăre, dedī, dătum = I give

doceō, -ēre, docuī, doctum = I teach

doleō, -ēre, doluī, dolitum = I feel pain, am sad

dolor, dolōris, m. = pain, grief

dolus, -ī, m. = trick

domesticus, -a, -um = of the household, domestic

domicilium, -iī, n. = dwelling, house

dominus, -ī, m. = master, lord

domō (abl. of **domus**) = from home

domum (acc. of **domus**) = homewards

domus, -ūs, f. (irreg.) = house, home

dōnum, -ī, n. = gift

dormiō, -īre, -īvī, -ītum = I sleep

dubitō, -āre, -āvī, -ātum = I doubt, hesitate

dubium, -ī, n. = doubt

dūcō, -ere, dūxī, ductum = I lead, spin (wool)

dum = while

duŏ, duae, duŏ = two

duodecim = twelve

duodēvīgintī = eighteen

duplicō, -āre, -āvī, -ātum = I double, copy

dūrus, -a, -um = hard

dux, ducis, c. = leader

dūxī: see **dūcō**

ē, ex (+ abl.) = out of

eam = her

eās = them (feminine)

ēbrius, -a, -um = drunk

ecce = look!

edō, ēsse (or **edere**)**, ēdī, ēsum** (irreg.) = I eat

ēdūcō, -ere, ēdūxī, ēductum = I lead out

effluō, -ere, effūxī = I flow out

effugiō, -ere, effūgī = I escape

effundō, -ere, effūdī, effūsum = I pour forth

ēgī: see **agō**

egŏ = I

ēheu = alas

ēleganter = elegantly

emō, emere, ēmī, ēmptum = I buy

enim = for (not written 1st word in clause)

eō = to that place (thither)

eō, īre, iī (or **īvī**), **itum** (irreg.) = I go

eōs = them, those (masculine plural)

equus, equī, m. = horse

ēripiō, -ere, ēripuī, ēreptum = I snatch away

errō, -āre, -āvī, -ātum = I wander, make a mistake

ērudītus, -a, -um = learned

esse: see **sum**

et = and

et...et = both...and

etiam = even, also

eum = him

ēvādō, -ere, ēvāsī, ēvāsum = I escape

ex (+ abl.) = out of

excavō, -āre, -āvī, -ātum = I hollow out

excitō, -āre, -āvī, -ātum = I waken, excite

exclāmō, -āre, -āvī, -ātum = I shout out

excolō, -ere, excoluī, excultum = I improve

exeō, exīre, exiī, exitum (goes like **eō**) = I go out

exerceō, -ēre, -uī, -itum = I exercise

exitium, -ī, n. = destruction

exquīsītus, -a, -um = exquisite, refined

exstīnctus, -a, -um = exstinguished, put out

exsul, exsulis, m. = exile

exspectō, -āre, -āvī, -ātum = I wait for

exuō, -ere, exuī, exūtum = I take off

extrā (+ acc.) = outside

fābula, -ae, f. = story

facile (adverb) = easily

facilis, -e = easy

faciō, -ere, fēci, factum = I do, make

falsus, -a, -um = untrue, false

fāma, -ae, f. = fame, glory

famulus, -ī, m. = household slave

fātidicus, -a, -um = prophetic

fātum, -ī, n. = fate, destiny

faveō, -ēre, fāvī, fautum (+ dat.) = I favour

fēcī: see ***faciō***

fēlīciter (adverb) = fortunately, happily

fēlīx, fēlīcis = fortunate, happy

fēmina, -ae, f. = woman

fenestra, -ae, f. = window

fera, -ae, f. = wild beast

ferō, ferre, tulī, lātum (irreg.) = I carry, bear

ferōx, ferōcis = fierce, spirited

fessus, -a, -um = tired

festīnō, -āre, -āvī, -ātum = I hurry

fēstus, -a, -um = festive

fidēlis, -e = faithful

fīdus, -a, -um = trustworthy, safe

figūra, -ae, f. = form, shape

fīlia, -ae, f. = daughter (dat. and abl. pl.: ***fīliābus***)

fīlius, fīliī (or ***fīlī***), m. (irreg.) = son

fīxus, -a, -um = fixed

flagellum, -ī, n. = whip

flamma, -ae, f. = flame

flōs, flōris, m. = flower

flūmen, flūminis, n. = river

fluvius, -ī, m. = river

focus, -ī, m. = hearth

folium, -ī, n. = leaf

fōrma, -ae, f. = shape, beauty, form

fortasse = perhaps

forte = by chance

fortūna, -ae, f. = fortune

forum, -ī, n. = forum

frangō, -ere, frēgī, frāctum = I break

frāter, frātris, m. = brother

fraudō, -āre, -āvī, -ātum = I cheat

fraudulentus, -a, -um = fraudulent

frēgī: see ***frangō***

frīgidus, -a, -um = cold

frūstrā = in vain

fuga, -ae, f. = flight, escape

fugiō, -ere, fūgī, fugitum = I flee (from)

fuī: see ***sum***

fulgeō, -ēre, fūlsī = I flash, glitter, shine

fulmen, fulminis, n. = thunderbolt

fūmus, -ī, m. = smoke

fungus, -ī, m. = mushroom

fūr, fūris, m. = thief

futūrum, -ī, n. = the future

galea, -ae, f. = helmet

Gallia, -ae, f. = Gaul (the country)

Gallus, -ī, m. = a Gaul (the person)

garrulus, -a, -um = talkative, chattering

garum, -ī, n. = fish-sauce

gaudium, gaudiī, n. = joy

gemō, -ere, -uī, -itum = I groan

gena, -ae, f. = cheek

gerō, -ere, gessī, gestum = I manage, wear

gessī: see ***gerō***

gladius, gladiī, m. = sword

glōria, -ae, f. = glory

gradus, gradūs, m. = step

Graecia, -ae, f. = Greece

Graecus, -a, -um = Greek

grātiam habeō = I am grateful

grātiās agō = I give thanks

grātus, -a, -um = welcome, pleasing

gravis, -e = heavy, serious

habeō, -ēre, -uī, -itum = I have, I consider

habitō, -āre, -āvī, -ātum = I live, inhabit

haesitō, -āre, -āvī, -ātum = I hesitate

harēna, -ae, f. = sand, arena

hasta, -ae, f. = spear

herba, -ae, f. = grass

herī = yesterday

hībernus, -a, -um = wintry, belonging to winter

hīc = here

hic, haec, hoc = this; he, she, it

hiems, hiemis, f. = winter, stormy weather

hinnītus, -ūs, m. = neighing

hirsūtus, -a, -um = hairy

hodiē = today

homŏ, hominis, c. = person, man

hōra, -ae, f. = hour

hortus, -ī, m. = garden

hospes, hospitis, m. = host, guest

hospitium, -ī, n. = hospitality

hostis, hostis, c. = enemy (of the state; usually used in plural)

hūmānus, -a, -um = human

hūmidus, -a, -um = damp

humō, -āre, -āvī, -ātum = I bury

iaceō, -ēre, iacuī, iacitum = I lie (down)

iaciō, -ere, iēcī, iactum = I throw

iam = now, already

iānua, -ae, f. = door

ibĭ = there

Icēnī, -ōrum, m. pl. = Iceni (a tribe in Britain)

iēcī: see *iaciō*

igitur = therefore (not generally written 1st word in clause)

ignārus, -a, -um = ignorant, unaware

ignis, ignis, m. (abl. sing.: *ignī* or *igne*) = fire

ignōrō, -āre, -āvī, -ātum = I do not know

ille = that man, he

illūminō, -āre, -āvī, -ātum = I light up

immōtus, -a, -um = motionless

impediō, -īre, -īvī, -ītum = I hinder

imperātor, -ōris, m. = general

imperium, -ī, n. = command, empire

implōrō, -āre, -āvī, -ātum = I beg, beseech

impluvium, -ī, n. = impluvium (a basin in the floor of the atrium for catching rain-water)

imprūdēns, -entis = unwise

in (+ abl.) = in, on

in (+ acc.) = into, on to

incendium, -ī, n. = fire

incendō, -ere, incendī, incēnsum = I burn (transitive)

incitō, -āre, -āvī, -ātum = I set in motion

incola, -ae, c. = inhabitant

incolō, -ere, incoluī = I inhabit

inde = then, thence

induō, -ere, induī, indūtum = I put on

indūtus, -a, -um = dressed, clad

īnfāns, -antis, c. = a little child

īnfēlīx, -īcis = unfortunate

īnferior, -ōris = lower

īnfernus, -a, -um = lower, underground

īnfirmus, -a, -um = feeble

īnflammō, -āre, -āvī, -ātum = I set on fire

īnfrā + acc. = beneath

ingenium, -ī, n. = ability (of intellect)

ingeniōsus, -a, -um = clever

iniciō, -ere, iniēcī, iniectum = I throw

iniūria, -ae, f. = injustice, wrong, harm

iniūstus, -a, -um = unjust

innoxius, -a, -um = harmless

inquit / inquiunt = he/they say(s) (quoting direct speech)

īnsānia, -ae, f. = insanity
īnsānus, -a, -um = insane
īnsula, -ae, f. = island, block of flats
integer, -gra, -grum = whole
intellegō, -ere, intellēxī, intellēctum = I understand
inter (+ acc.) = between, among
interficiō, -ere, interfēcī, interfectum = I kill
interrogō, -āre, -āvī, -ātum = I ask, interrogate
intrā (+ acc.) = within
intrō, -āre, -āvī, -ātum = I enter
inveniō, -īre, invēnī, inventum = I find
investīgō, -āre, -āvī, -ātum = I find out
invītō, -āre, -āvī, -ātum = I invite
invītus, -a, -um = unwilling, reluctant
involvō, -ere, involvī, involūtum = I wrap
Iovem: see *Iuppiter*
ipse, ipsa, ipsum = self
īra, -ae, f. = anger
īrātus, -a, -um = angry
irrigō, -āre, -āvī, -ātum = I water, irrigate
ita = thus
Ītalia, -ae, f. = Italy
Ītalicus, -a, -um = Italian
itaque = therefore
iter, itineris, n. = journey
iterō, -āre, -āvī, -ātum = I repeat
iterum = again
iubeō, -ēre, iussī, iussum = I order
Iuppiter, Iovis, m. = Jupiter
iussī: see *iubeō*
iussum, -ī, n. = an order
iussus: see *iubeō*
iūstitia, -ae, f. = justice
iūstus, -a, -um = just, righteous
iuvenis, iuvenis, c. = young person, young man
iuvō, iuvāre, iūvī, iūtum = I help

labor, labōris, m. = work, task
labōrō, -āre, -āvī, -ātum = I work
labrum, -ī, n. = lip
labyrinthus, -ī, m. = labyrinth, maze
lacerna, -ae, f. = cloak
lacerō, -āre, -āvī, -ātum = I tear to pieces
lacrima, -ae, f. = tear
lacrimō, -āre, -āvī, -ātum = I weep, cry
lacus, -ūs, m. = lake
laetus, -a, -um = happy
lambō, -ere, lambī, lambitum = I lick
lāna, -ae, f. = wool
languidus, -a, -um = weak, feeble, sluggish
lāserpīcium, -ī, n. = silphium (a medicinal herb)
lateō, -ēre, latuī = I lie hidden
lātrō, -āre, -āvī, -ātum = I bark
lātus, -a, -um = wide
laudō, -āre, -āvī, -ātum = I praise
laurus, -ī, f. = laurel, bay tree
lavō, -āre, lāvī, lautum (or *lavātum*) = I wash
laxō, -āre, -āvī, -ātum = I loosen, relax
lectus, -ī, m. = bed, couch
legiō, -ōnis, f. = legion
legō, -ere, lēgī, lēctum = I read, choose
lēns, lentis, f. = lentil
lentē = slowly
levis, -e = light, unimportant
libenter = gladly, willingly
līber, -era, -erum = free
liber, librī, m. = book
līberālitās, -ātis, f. = generosity
līberī, -ōrum, m. pl. = offspring, children (of someone)
līberō, -āre, -āvī, -ātum = I free
ligneus, -a, -um = wooden
ligō, -āre, -āvī, -ātum = I bind, tie
lingua, -ae, f. = tongue, language

līnum, -ī, n. = thread
liquidus, -a, -um = liquid
locus, -ī, m. = place
longus, -a, -um = long
lūdō, -ere, lūsī, lūsum = I play
lūdus, -ī, m. = school, game
lūgeō, -ēre, lūxī, lūctum = I mourn, grieve
lūmen, lūminis, n. = light
lūna, -ae, f. = moon
lupa, -ae, f. = she-wolf
lūsī: see *lūdō*
lūx, lūcis, f. = light
lyra, -ae, f. = lyre
māchina, -ae, f. = machine, engine
maereō, -ēre = I mourn, am sad
maestus, -a, um = sad
magister, magistrī, m. = master, schoolmaster
magnopere = greatly
magnus, -a, -um = big, great
malus, -a, -um = bad
maneō, -ēre, mānsī, mānsum = I remain
manus, -ūs, f. = hand, (or band of men)
mappa, -ae, f. = cloth, napkin
marītus, -ī, m. = husband
māter, mātris, f. = mother
mathēmaticus, -ī, m. = mathematician
mātrimōnium, -iī, n. = marriage
mātrōna, -ae, f. = married woman
mātūrus, -a, -um = ripe
maximus, -a, -um = biggest, greatest
mē: me (see *egǒ*)
medicīna, -ae, f. = medicine
medicus, -ī, m. = doctor
medius, -a, -um = middle
mel, mellis, n. = honey
melior, -us = better
mēns, mentis, f. = mind
mēnsa, mēnsae, f. = table
mēnsis, mēnsis, m. = month

meus, -a, -um = my
migrō, -āre, -āvī, -ātum = I go away, migrate, change home
mihǐ = to me (dative of *egǒ*)
mīles, mīlitis, c. = soldier
mīlia, mīlium, n. pl. (+ gen.) = thousands
mīlle = one thousand
minimē = very little
minimus, -a, -um = smallest
minor, minus = smaller
Mīnōtaurus, -ī, m. = Minotaur
minus = less
mīrāculum, -ī, n. = miracle
mīrus, -a, -um = marvellous, amazing
miser, -era, -erum = wretched
misericordia, -ae, f. = pity
mīsī: see *mittō*
mittō, -ere, mīsī, missum = I send, throw (a missile)
modestia, -ae, f. = modesty
modus, -ī, m. = way, manner
moenia, moenium, n. pl. = fortified walls, ramparts
moneō, -ēre, -uī, -itum = I warn, advise
mōns, montis, m. = mountain
mōnstrō, -āre, -āvī, -ātum = I show, point out
morbus, -ī, m. = disease
mors, mortis, f. = death
mortālis, -e = mortal
mortuus, -a, -um = dead
mōs, mōris, m. = custom
moveō, -ēre, mōvī, mōtum = I move (transitive)
mox = soon
mulier, mulieris, f. = woman
mulsum, -ī, n. = honey-wine
multitūdō, multitūdinis, f. = crowd, multitude
multum (adverb) = much
multus, -a, -um = much, many
mūniō, -īre, -īvī, -ītum = I fortify

murmur, murmuris, n. = murmuring
mūrus, -ī, m. = wall
mūsicus, -ī, m. = musician
mūtō, -āre, -āvī, -ātum = I change
nam = for
narcissus, -ī, m. = narcissus
nārrō, -āre, -āvī, -ātum = I tell
nāsus, ī, m. = nose
natō, -āre, -āvī, -ātum = I swim
nātūra, -ae, f. = nature
nātus, -a, -um = born
nauta, -ae, m. = sailor
nāvigō, -āre, -āvī, -ātum = I sail
-ne?: introduces a question
nec = and not, nor
nec tamen = but…not
nec…nec = neither…nor
necessārius, -a, -um = necessary
necō, necāre, necāvī, necātum = I kill
neglegō, -ere, neglēxī, neglēctum = I neglect
negō, -āre, -āvī, -ātum = I deny, say that…not
negōtium, -iī, n. = business, work
nēmō, (nēminem, nūllǐus, nēminī, nūllō), c. = no one
neque = and not, nor
neque tamen = but…not
neque…neque = neither…nor
nesciǒ, -īre, -īvī, -ītum = I do not know
nihil (or **nīl**) = nothing, in no way
nisi (or **nī**) = unless, if…not, except
nitidus, -a, -um = shining, bright
nōbilis, -e = noble, famous
nōbīs = to us (dative of **nōs**)
nōlō, nōlle, nōluī (irreg.) = I do not wish, am unwilling
nōmen, nōminis, n. = name
nōn = not
nōn diūtius = not for a longer time
nōn iam = no longer
nōn sōlum…sed etiam = not only…but also

nōnne?: introduces a question (expecting the answer "yes")
nōs = we
noster, nostra, nostrum = our
notō, -āre, -āvī, -ātum = I mark
nōtus, -a, -um = well-known
novem = nine
novus, -a, -um = new
nox, noctis, f. = night
nūbēs, -is, f. = cloud
nūdō, -āre, -āvī, -ātum = I uncover
nūdus, -a, -um = naked
nūllus, -a, -um (like **ūnus**) = no (adjective)
num?: introduces a question (expecting the answer "no")
numerus, ī, m. = number
numerō, -āre, -āvī, -ātum = I count
numquam = never
nunc = now
nūntiō, -āre, -āvī, -ātum = I report, announce
nūntius, nūntiī, m. = messenger, message
nūper = recently
nux, nucis, f. = nut
nympha, -ae, f. = nymph
obdormīscō, -ere, obdormīvī = I go to sleep
obsideō, -ēre, obsēdī, obsessum = I blockade
obstinātus, -a, -um = obstinate
occupātus, -a, -um = busy
octǒ = eight
octǒgintā = eighty
oculus, -ī, m. = eye
odor, -ōris, m. = smell
offendō, -ere, offendī, offēnsum = I offend
oleum, -ī, n. = oil
ōlim = once upon a time
olīva, -ae, f. = olive
olla, -ae, f. = pot
omnēs (nom., voc. and acc. pl.) = all
omnipotēns, -entis = all-powerful

omnis, -e = every, all

onus, oneris, n. = burden

oppidum, -ī, n. = town

opprimō, -ere, oppressī, oppressum = I overwhelm, oppress

oppugnō, -āre, -āvī, -ātum = I attack (a town or city)

optimus, -a, -um = best

optō, -āre, -āvī, -ātum = I wish, choose

opulentus, -a, -um = rich

opus, operis, n. = work

ōra, -ae, f. = shore

ōrāculum, -ī, n. = oracle

ōrātor, -ōris, m. = orator

ōrnō, -āre, -āvī, -ātum = I adorn, decorate

ōrō, -āre, -āvī, -ātum = I beg, pray

ōsculum, -ī, n. = kiss

ōvum, -ī, n. = egg

Padus, -ī, m. = River Po

paene = almost

palaestra, -ae, f. = exercise-ground

Palātium, -iī, m. = the Palatine Hill

palla, -ae, f. = palla (a woman's cloak)

palleō, -ēre, -uī = I grow pale

palma, -ae, f. = palm

pānis, pānis, m. = bread

pāreō, -ēre, -uī, -itum (+ dat.) = I obey

pariō, -ere, peperī, partum (or *paritum*) = I give birth to, produce, (of victories =) I win

parō, -āre, -āvī, -ātum = I prepare

pars, partis, f. = part

parvus, -a, -um = small

pater, patris, m. = father

paterfamiliās = head of the household (n.b. *familiās* is an archaic genitive of the noun *familiā*)

patria, -ae, f. = country, fatherland

pauper, pauperis (like *vetus*) = poor

peccō, -āre, -āvī, -ātum = I sin

pecūnia, -ae, f. = money

pellō, -ere, pepulī, pulsum = I drive

Penātēs, -ium, m. pl. = the Penates (household gods)

peperī: see *pariō*

per (+ acc.) = through, along

pereō, -īre, periī, peritum (goes like *eō*) = I die

perfidia, -ae, f. = treachery

perīculum, -ī, n. = danger

peristylium, -ī, n. = internal court sorrounded by pillars

perturbō, -āre, -āvī, -ātum = I throw into confusion

pēs, pedis, m. = foot

pestilentia, -ae, f. = pestilence, plague

petō, -ere, petīvī, petītum (+ acc.) = I seek, I make for; (+ *ā/ab* + abl.) = I ask

philosophus, -ī, m. = philosopher

pictūra, -ae, f. = picture

pilleus, -ī, m. = felt cap

pinna, -ae, f. = feather

piscātor, -ōris, m. = fisherman

piscīna, -ae, f. = swimming-pool

piscis, -is, m. = fish

placeō, placēre, placuī, placitum (+ dat.) = I please

plācō, -āre, -āvī, -ātum = I calm

plaustrum, -ī, n. = cart

plēctrum, -ī, n. = plectrum (small stick for playing a stringed instrument)

plēnus, -a, -um (+ abl. or gen.) = full

plērumque = generally

pluit = it rains

plūrimus, -a, -um = most

plūs, plūris = more (neuter noun in singular; adjective in plural)

pluviae, -ārum, f. pl. = rains

pluvius, -a, -um = rainy

pōculum, -ī, n. = cup

poena, -ae, f. = penalty, punishment

poēta, -ae, m. = poet
pompa, -ae, f. = display
pōmum, -ī, n. = apple
pondus, ponderis, n. = weight
pōnō, -ere, posuī, positum = I
    place
pōns, pontis, m. = bridge
populus, -ī, m. = a people,
    population
porcus, -ī, m. = pig
porta, -ae, f. = gate
portentum, -ī, n. = portent
portō, -āre, -āvī, -ātum = I carry
possum, posse, potuī (irreg.) =
    I am able
post (+ acc.) = after, behind
posteā = afterwards
posuī: see ***pōnō***
potentia, -ae, f. = power
poterat/poterant/poteris: parts of
    possum
pōtō, -āre, -āvī, -ātum = I drink
potuī: see ***possum***
praebeō, -ēre, praebuī, praebitum
    = I offer, show
praedīcō, -ere, -dīxī, -dictum =
    I predict
praesertim = especially
praetereā = besides, in addition
prīdiē = the day before
prīmum = first (adverb)
prīmus, -a, -um = first
prīnceps, prīncipis, m. = chief,
    emperor
prō (+ abl.) = on behalf of, in place
    of, in front of, instead of
probus, -a, -um = honest, upright
prōcēdō, -ere, prōcessī,
    prōcessum = I go forward
procul = far away
prōdō, -ere, prōdidī, prōditum =
    I betray
proelium, -iī, n. = battle
prohibeō, -ēre, -uī, -itum =
    I prevent

prōmittō, -ere, prōmīsī,
    prōmissum = I promise
prōnus, -a, -um = prone
prope (+ acc.) = near
propinquī, -ōrum, m. pl. = relations
propter (+ acc.) = on account of
prōvideō, -ēre, prōvīdī, prōvīsum
    = I foresee
prōvincia, -ae, f. = province
prōvocō, -āre, -āvī, -ātum =
    I challenge
proximus, -a, -um = next, nearest
prūdēns, prūdentis = sensible
prūdentia, -ae, f. = good sense,
    judgement
prūnum, -ī, n. = plum
pudor, -ōris, m. = shame
puella, -ae, f. = girl
puer, puerī, m. = boy
pugna, -ae, f. = battle, fight
pugnō, -āre, -āvī, -ātum = I fight
pulcher, pulchra, pulchrum =
    beautiful
pulsō, -āre, -āvī, -ātum = I beat
pulvis, pulveris, m. = dust
pūniō, -īre, -īvī, -ītum = I punish
pūrgō, -āre, -āvī, -ātum = I clean
putŏ, -āre, -āvī, -ātum = I think
quadrāgintā = forty
quae: see ***quī***
quam (+ adjective or adverb) =
    how…!
quamquam = although
quantus, -a, -um? = how great?
quārtus, -a, -um = fourth
quattuor = four
quattuordecim = fourteen
-que = and
quī, quae, quod (relative pronoun) =
    who, which
quid? = what?, why?
quīndecim = fifteen
quīnquāgintā = fifty
quīnque = five
quīntus, -a, -um = fifth

quis? = who?

quō? = where to? (whither?)

quod = because

quōmodŏ? = how?

quoque = also (comes *after* the word it is emphasising)

quōrum = gen. pl. of *quī*

radius, -ī, m. = ray

rapidus, -a, -um = rapid

rapiō, -ere, rapuī, raptum = I seize

rārus, -a, -um = rare, far apart

recitō, -āre, -āvī, -ātum = I recite

recreātus, -a, -um = revived, refreshed

recreō, -āre, -āvī, -ātum = I revive, refresh

rēctus, -a, -um = right, straight

recumbō, -ere, recubuī = I lie down

redūcō, -ere, redūxi, reductum = I lead back

rēgia, -ae, f. = palace

rēgīna, -ae, f. = queen

regiō, -ōnis, f. = area, region

rēgnō, -āre, -āvī, -ātum = I rule, reign

rēgnum, -ī, n. = kingdom

regō, -ere, rēxī, rēctum = I rule, direct

relevō, -āre, -āvī, -ātum = I relieve, lighten

relinquō, -ere, relīquī, relictum = I leave, abandon

reliquiae, -ārum, f. pl. = remains

reliquus, -a, -um = remaining

remedium, -ī, n. = cure, remedy

rēmigō, -āre, -āvī, -ātum = I row

removeō, -ēre, -mōvī, -mōtum = I remove

repōnō, -ere, reposuī, repositum = I put back

respiciō, -ere, respexī, respectum = I look back

respondeō, -ēre, respondī, respōnsum = I reply, answer

respōnsum, -ī, n. = answer

retineō, -ēre, -uī, retentum = I hold back

retrō = backwards

reveniō, -īre, revēnī, reventum = I return

revocō, -āre, -āvī, -ātum = I call back

rēx, rēgis, m. = king

rēxī: see *rego*

Rhēnus, -ī, m. = River Rhine

Rhodanus, -ī, m. = River Rhone

rīdeō, -ēre, rīsī, rīsum = I laugh at, smile

rigidus, -a, -um = stiff

rīpa, -ae, f. = riverbank

rīsus, -ūs, m. = laughter

rogō, -āre, -āvī, -ātum = I ask

Rōma, -ae, f. = Rome

Rōmānus, -a, -um = Roman (adjective)

Rōmānus, -ī, m. = a Roman (noun)

roseus, -a, -um = rose-coloured

rōstrum, -ī, m. = beak

rūfus, -a, -um = red, reddish

rūricola, -ae, c. = a country-dweller

rūs, rūris, n. = the countryside

rūsticus, -a, -um = rustic, rural

sacrificō, -āre, -āvī, -ātum = I sacrifice

saepe = often

sagitta, -ae, f. = arrow

sagittārius, -ī, m. = archer

sal, salis, m. = salt

saliō, -īre, saluī, saltum = I leap, jump

salūtō, -āre, -āvī, -ātum = I greet

salvē, salvēte = hello, greetings

salvus, -a, -um = safe

sānitās, -ātis, f. = good health

sānō, -āre, -āvī, -ātum = I cure, heal

sānus, -a, -um = healthy, sane

sapientia, -ae, f. = wisdom

satis = enough

satyrus, -ī, m. = satyr (a wood deity with a horse's tail)

saxum, -ī, n. = rock
scientia, -ae, f. = knowledge
sciŏ, scīre, scīvī, scītum = I know
scrībō, -ere, scrīpsī, scrīptum = I
    write
scūtum, -ī, n. = shield
sē = himself, herself, itself,
    themselves
secundus, -a, -um = following,
    favourable
sed = but
sēdecim = sixteen
sedeō, sedēre, sēdī, sessum = I sit
sella, -ae, f. = chair, seat
semper = always
senātor, -ōris, m. = senator
senex, senis, m. = old man
senior, -ōris, c. = elderly person
sentiō, -īre, sēnsī, sēnsum = I feel,
    notice, realise
sepeliō, -īre, sepelīvī, sepultum =
    I bury
septem = seven
septendecim = seventeen
septimus = seventh
sepulcrum, -ī, n. = tomb
serēnus, -a, -um = calm
sērō = late
serpēns, -entis, c. = serpent, snake
servō, -āre, -āvī, -ātum = I save
servus, -ī, m. = slave
sēstertius, -iī, m. (gen. pl.:
    sēstertium) = sestertius
    (Roman coin)
sex = six
sextus, -a, -um = sixth
sī = if
sīc = thus
siccus, -a, -um = dry
sīcut = just as
significō, -āre, -āvī, -ātum = I signify
signum, -ī, n. = signal, sign
silva, -ae, f. = wood, forest
similis, -e (+ dat. or gen.) = similar
    (to), like

simul = at the same time
simulō, -āre, -āvī, -ātum = I pretend
sine (+ abl.) = without
sinister, -tra, -trum = left, on the left
sinistra, -ae, f. = left hand
sinistrā = on the left
sinō, -ere, sīvī, situm = I allow
socius, -iī, m. = ally
sōl, sōlis, m. = sun
solidus, -a, -um = solid
sōlum (adverb) = only
sōlus, -a, -um (like *ūnus*) = alone
solvō, -ere, solvī, solūtum =
    I release, let loose, pay
somnium, -iī, n. = dream
somnus, -ī, m. = sleep
sonō, -āre, sonuī, sonitum = I
    make a sound
sonus, -ī, m. = sound
soror, -ōris, f. = sister
spectāculum, -ī, n. = spectacle
spectō, -āre, -āvī, -ātum = I watch
spērō, -āre, -āvī, -ātum = I hope,
    look for
sphaera, -ae, f. = sphere
spīrō, -āre, -āvī, -ātum = I breathe
splendidus, -a, -um = brilliant,
    gleaming
stabulum, -ī, n. = stable
stāgnum, -ī, n. = pool
statim = immediately
statua, -ae, f. = statue
stēlla, -ae, f. = star
sternuō, -ere, sternuī = I sneeze
stetī: see *stō*
stō, stāre, stetī, stătum = I stand
stola, -ae, f. = dress
strangulō, -āre, -āvī, -ātum =
    I throttle
strēnuus, -a, -um = active,
    energetic
studeō, -ēre, -uī (+ dat.) = I study,
    apply myself (to), am eager
    about
stultus, -a, -um = stupid

sub (+ abl.) = under
subitō = suddenly
submergō, -ere, submersī, submersum = I submerge, cause to drown
sum, esse, fuī (irreg.) = I am
summa, -ae, f. = sum, total, amount
sūmō, -ere, sūmpsī, sūmptum = I take up, assume
sūmptuōsus, -a, -um = expensive, extravagent
super (+ acc.) = over
superbia, -ae, f. = pride
superbus, -a, -um = proud
superō, -āre, -āvī, -ātum = I overcome
supplicium, -ī, n. = punishment
suprā + acc. = above
surgō, -ere, surrēxī, surrēctum = I rise, get up
suscipiō, -ere, suscēpī, susceptum = I undertake
suspīciōsus, -a, -um = suspicious
sustineō, -ēre, sustinuī, sustentum = I hold up, hold back
susurrus, -ī, m. = whispering
suus, sua, suum = his (own), her (own), its (own) or their (own)
Syrācūsae, -ārum, f. pl. = Syracuse
Syrācūsānus, -a, -um = Syracusan
taberna, -ae, f. = inn, shop
taceō, -ēre, tacuī, tacitum = I am silent
tacitus, -a, -um = silent
taeda, -ae, f. = pine torch
taedet = it wearies
tam = so
tamen = however (not generally written first word in clause)
Tamesis, -is, m. (acc. sing.: *Tamesim*) = River Thames
tandem = at last
tangō, tangere, tetigī, tāctum = I touch
tantus, -a, -um = so great

tēctum, -ī, n. = roof
tēlum, -ī, n. = spear, missile
tempestās, -ātis, f. = storm, weather
templum, -ī, n. = temple
temptō, -āre, -āvī, -ātum = I try
tempus, -ŏris, n. = time
tenebrae, -ārum, f. pl. = darkness
teneō, -ēre, tenuī, tentum = I hold
tener, -era, -erum = tender, young
tepidārium, -ī, n. = warm room (in the baths)
ter = three times
terra, -ae, f. = land, earth
terreō, -ēre, -uī, -itum = I terrify
territus, -a, -um = terrified
tertius, -a, -um = third
testāmentum, -ī, n. = will
tetigī: see *tangō*
textum, ī, n. = woven cloth
textus, -a, -um = woven
theātrum, -ī, n. = theatre
thermae, -ārum, f. pl. = baths
tiāra, -ae, f. = head-dress, turban
Tiber, Tiberis, m. (acc. sing.: *Tiberim*) = River Tiber
tibĭ (dat. of *tū*) = to you
tībia, -ae, f. = shin-bone, flute
timeō, -ēre, -uī = I fear
timidus, -a, -um = timid
timor, -ōris, m. = fear
toga, -ae, f. = toga
tolerō, -āre, -āvī, -ātum = I tolerate
tondeō, -ēre, totondī, tōnsum = I shave
tonō, -āre, tonuī = I thunder
tōtus, -a, -um (like *ūnus*) = whole
trādō, -ere, trādidī, trāditum = I hand over
trahō, -ere, trāxī, tractum = I drag
tranquillus, -a, -um = quiet, peaceful
trāns (+ acc.) = across
trānsferō, -ferre, -tulī, -lātum = transfer, carry across

trānsfīxus, -a, -um = pierced
trāxī: see **trahō**
trecentī, -ae, -a = three hundred
tredecim = thirteen
trepidō, -āre, -āvī, -ātum = I tremble
trepidus, -a, -um = trembling
trēs, tria = three
trīclīnium, -ī, n. = dining-room
trīgintā = thirty
triumphālis, -e = triumphal
Troia, -ae, f. = Troy (note that the 'o' of **Troia** is pronounced short)
Troiānus, -a, -um = Trojan
tū = you (singular)
tulī: see **ferō**
tum = then, at that time
tumultus, -ūs, m. = uproar, riot
tunica, -ae, f. = tunic
turba, -ae, f. = crowd
turbō, -āre, -āvī, -ātum = I disturb
Tuscus, -a, -um = Etruscan
tūtus, -a, -um = safe
tuus, -a, -um = your (belonging to you (sing.))
ubĭ = when; where
ubĭ? = where?
ūllus, -a, -um (like **ūnus**) = any
ululō, -āre, -āvī, -ātum = I howl
umbra, -ae, f. = shadow
umerus, -ī, m. = shoulder
ūmidus, -a, -um = damp
unda, -ae, f. = wave
ūndecim = eleven
ūndēvīgintī = nineteen
ungō, -ere, ūnxī, ūnctum = I smear with oil
unguentum, -ī, n. = scented oil, perfume
ūnus, -a, -um (gen. sing.: **ūnĭus**, dat. sing.: **ūnī**) = one, only one, one alone
urbānitās, -ātis, f. = courtesy
urbānus, -a, -um = polite
urbs, urbis, f. = city
urna, -ae, f. = urn

ursa, -ae, f. = she-bear
ut = as
ūtilis, -e = useful
uxor, -ōris, f. = wife
vae = alas
valē / valēte = farewell
valeō, -ēre, valuī, valitum = I am strong, healthy, able
validus, -a, -um = strong
vapor, -ōris, m. = steam
varius, -a, -um = various, different
vastātiō, -ōnis, f. = devastation
vastō, -āre, -āvī, -ātum = I lay waste, devastate
vehō, -ere, vēxī, vectum = I convey
vel…vel = either…or
velle: see **volō**
vēndō, -ere, vēndidī, vēnditum = I sell
veniō, -īre, vēnī, ventum = I come
venter, ventris, m. = stomach
ventus, -ī, m. = wind
vēr, vēris, n. = spring
verberō, -āre, -āvī, -ātum = I flog, whip
verbum, -ī, n. = word
vērus -a, -um = true
vester, vestra, vestrum = your (belonging to you (pl.))
vestibulum, -ī, n. = enclosed entrance
vestīgium, -ī, n. = foot-print, trace
vestīmentum, -ī, n. = clothing
vestis, vestis, f. = clothing
vetō, vetāre, vetuī, vetitum = I forbid
vetus, veteris = old
vexō, -āre, -āvī, -ātum = I annoy
via, -ae, f. = road, street, way
vibrō, -āre, -āvī, -ātum = I move to and fro, shake
vīcīnus, -a, -um = neighbouring
vīcīnus, -ī, m. = neighbour
victor, -ōris, m. = victor
victōria, -ae, f. = victory

victōriam pariō = I win a victory

videō, -ēre, vīdī, vīsum = I see

vidua, -ae, f. = widow

vīgintī = twenty

vīlla, -ae, f. = country house, villa

vincō, -ere, vīcī, victum = I conquer

vīnum, -ī, n. = wine

viola, -ae, f. = violet

violentia, -ae, f. = violence

violentus, -a, -um = violent

vir, virī, m. (irreg.) = man (as opposed to woman)

virga, -ae, f. = rod, stick

vīsitō, -āre, -āvī, -ātum = I visit

vīta, -ae, f. = life

vītō, -āre, -āvī, -ātum = I avoid

vīvō, vīvere, vīxī, vīctum = I live, am alive

vīvus, -a, -um = alive

vix = scarcely

vōbīs = to you (dative plural of *vōs*)

vocō, -āre, -āvī, -ātum = I call

volō, -āre, -āvī, -ātum = I fly

volō, velle, voluī (irreg.) = I wish, am willing

Volscī, -ōrum, m. pl. = the Volsci (a tribe in Italy)

vōs = you (plural)

vōx, vōcis, f. = voice

vulnerō, -āre, -āvī, -ātum = I wound